Stick Happy Debt Collectors

Allen Harkleroad

Statesboro Georgia, USA

Edited by Bill James

Copyright © 2010 Allen Harkleroad
All rights reserved. No part of this publication may be reproduced or transmitted in any form or by any means, electronic or mechanical, including photocopy, recording, or any information storage and retrieval system, without permission in writing from the copyright owner.

ISBN: 0-9789997-2-x

ISBN13: 978-0-9789997-2-8

Printed in the United States of America.

Legal information is not legal advice

STICK IT TO SUE HAPPY DEBT COLLECTORS

Other books by Allen Harkleroad
Confidential SEO Secrets
The Care and Feeding of a Sucks.com

Foreword

Collections lawsuits are big business. If you want to see just how often debt collectors sue consumers, go down to just about any courthouse in America and watch. At the motions docket call, you can watch as attorneys for debt collectors, take default judgment after default judgment against consumers who have not shown up to protect themselves.

I have sat in courtrooms from New Hampshire to Alabama and about everywhere in between, and watched defaults be granted often ten or twenty at a time. It's the same attorney, same bank as plaintiff, only the name of the consumer changes, and is little noticed by anyone in the courtroom. The sheer numbers of these lawsuits are staggering. If you have been sued by collectors you certainly are not alone.

By not appearing in the action, or not showing up in Court, you just make it easy for the collectors. Even if they have no proof, or you never owed the amount claimed, once the collectors get a judgment against you attacking the underlying debt becomes much more difficult. Even worse, once the debt has been legitimized by the Court system through the judgment, in many cases the collectors then have the ability to have law enforcement seize your assets and garnish your wages.

Once that has happened, an argument that you do not owe the

STICK IT TO SUE HAPPY DEBT COLLECTORS

debt or that it is for a different amount will often fall on deaf ears. You need to protect your rights and the information in this book can help you do it. While going to Court, or even just the idea of going to Court can be intimidating, many who have put aside their fears and raised their hand to protect themselves, end up being pleasantly surprised at what they are able to accomplish. It is empowering for many.

Remember the Judges are either elected by you or appointed by those that are. I have often seen judges give a self represented consumer considerable deference when they are up against big companies and their lawyers. You have nothing to lose by fighting. If you do not fight, the collectors win automatically. With a little time and effort you can put the tools learned from Allen's thousands of hours of research and experience fighting collections lawsuits to good use. Buying this book is a good start, keep going.

Allen Harkleroad may just be the most dangerous consumer in America for companies that treat people unfairly. He has a long and distinguished history of sticking it to those who have treated him and others unfairly, be it through his famous or infamous depending on whether your company has been targeted "sucks.com" sites or his experiences in battling some of the larg-

STICK IT TO SUE HAPPY DEBT COLLECTORS

est debt collectors on the planet. The only thing more surprising than the list of huge opponents he has taken on, are the results he consistently achieves with nothing other than hard work and a passion for standing up for what he believes in. Since unfortunate circumstances made him the target of debt collectors and their attorney's often unfair tactics and lawsuits, Allen has undertaken a crusade against the collectors.

As is his nature, Allen is not content to use his experiences and knowledge to help only himself. He wants ALL consumers to stand up to these companies and their lawyers. You can now take advantage of his thousands of hours of research and considerable experience and put it to good use in defending yourself against collections lawsuits. This book provides clear and practical advice that can be used by anyone who is targeted by debt collectors. It is up to you to put the advice to good use.

I sue debt collectors for treating consumers unfairly. Just because you may owe money does not give collectors or their attorneys the right to treat you unfairly. I talk to people every day about the tactics used by collectors and their lawyers against them, and hear amazing stories.

While you may think that being sued by the collector's falls into this category that is not often the case. There are situations

STICK IT TO SUE HAPPY DEBT COLLECTORS

where a debt collector can't call or send a letter to your house without violating the law, but nothing stops them from suing you. Further, rather than a lawsuit being the end of harassment -- that's what all those letters said "if you don't pay we may sue you" right? -- The lawsuit is often just the beginning of greater harassment to come. In the down economy there is more and more pressure on the banks and their collectors to get you to pay.

Further, with more people out of work and having trouble making ends meet, it is a growth industry with more and more collectors entering the marketplace and more accounts to collect on. The sad truth is that the collectors who are the most aggressive and use the most offensive tactics get paid first. This situation leads to the hardball tactics used by the collectors.

Worse yet consumers often find that they have nowhere to turn for help. Chances are that if they had the resources to pay an attorney hundreds of dollars an hour to represent them they would not have found themselves in the situation they need help with in the first place.

The collectors, often the biggest banks in the world, the same ones that the Government gave billions of tax dollars to this year, have unlimited funds to hire lawyers and go after consumers. Consumers help agencies have great intentions, but

STICK IT TO SUE HAPPY DEBT COLLECTORS

nowhere near the resources to help all of those in need.

Bottom line is that you as a consumer need to be prepared to stand up and assert your rights to protect yourself. With Allen on your side, you are on the right track.

By not fighting collections lawsuits, consumers are making the job of the collectors and their lawyers easier. If this trend continues the number of collections lawsuits will only increase.

You can fight and assert your rights. You can win. Go see for yourself. If you appear in Court to fight a debt collector's lawsuit, you will be one voice amongst the silent majority of consumers that do not stand up for themselves. Allen did a lot of the hard work for you. It is now up to you to put it to good use. As I noted above, you have nothing to lose and everything to gain. If you do not fight, if you do not stand up and assert your rights, they win by default. Don't make it easy for the collectors.

Chris Gleason, Esq.

www.Consumerhelp911.com

STICK IT TO SUE HAPPY DEBT COLLECTORS

Acknowledgements

This book is dedicated to my uncle Roy who was an attorney in Georgia and passed away in 2009. He always answered my legal questions and provided excellent advice.

I would like to thank several people, some are lawyers and some are regular people from various walks of life.

I would like to thank Christopher Gleason, a consumer protection attorney at The Rose Law Firm, PLLC. Our many conversations regarding consumer debt led to the writing this book. Many times Chris would point me in the right direction when I inevitably came to a dead end; Chris has a real passion for protecting consumers from unscrupulous debt collectors.

Many thanks to Joseph Segui, a consumer protection attorney in Waynesville Georgia, for his help in assisting me in the final settlement stages of the FDCPA lawsuits that I filed against several debt collection companies. Joseph really goes to "bat" for consumers.

I would like to thank Peggy Cherry for her insights regarding defending against debt collection law firms as a pro se consumer. Peggy developed a great idea regarding credit card companies' use of securities and receivables, which I eventually crafted into my Motion to Dismiss bombshell. Peggy is a judicious consumer, and enjoys sharing what she has learned with others.

Thanks also go to my good friend Bill James. Without your editing expertise and ideas this book would have never been published. Our conversations, whatever the subject, are great and insightful. I look forward to many more.

Lastly I would like to thank my cousin Keith, who is a criminal defense attorney in South Georgia, for his time in listening to me, and pointing me in the right direction concerning Georgia State Laws and his candid remarks regarding the debt collection industry.

Introduction

My name is Allen Harkleroad and I am not an attorney. The information in this book is for informational purposes and cannot in any way, shape or form be construed as legal advice. What you will read in my book is based on own personal experiences and what I've learned from dealing with debt collector lawsuits over the last couple of years. For the record, during this time I have been sued so many times over the last couple of years that I have literally lost count. The one thing I can tell you with one hundred percent certainty is this: I win in court and stick it to sue happy debt collectors, attorneys and law firms.

I look at being sued by a debt collector like this: If you are going to sue me, you better have the proof and documentation to validate it. I will fight and tooth and nail if the attorney or law firm can't or won't show proper proof. It doesn't matter if I owe the debt or not.

It took a while to learn out how to represent myself in court and win against lawsuit happy debt collection law firms and debt collection companies. Most consumers have no idea how to deal with debt lawsuits and most cannot afford the services of an attorney. This is why I wrote this book.

STICK IT TO SUE HAPPY DEBT COLLECTORS

The information shared with you in this book has been used by me and other consumers to win against debt collection lawsuits; simply put it works. It is not possible to guarantee these strategies, but I can say that with the exception of the first two debt lawsuits (where my learning began), none have gone past my Motion to Dismiss. After those two suits I decided I would learn how to fight a debt lawsuit and win. I have since learned how to get debt collectors, attorneys and the lawsuits to go away.

In this book, I will cover *original creditor lawsuits* and *junk debt buyer lawsuits* (3rd party collectors), and the similar ways that you will deal with them. I will also cover strategies to keep debt collectors off your back *before* any lawsuits are filed and how and when to sue a debt collector for violations of the Fair Debt Collection Practices Act (FDCPA) and the Fair Credit Reporting Act (FCRA).

My ultimate goal is to show you how to overwhelm the opposing attorney and to show them that, on their part, the burden of proving the debt is going to be an arduous, long, tiring and expensive journey. Most attorneys will bail out (voluntary dismissal) once they see that they must spend time and money to prove the case. I am not an "easy money target" and after you read my book neither will you.

STICK IT TO SUE HAPPY DEBT COLLECTORS

As a consumer I have a very low regard for debt collection attorneys and law firms that file an enormous volume of debt lawsuits. These questionable attorneys are betting the odds that you won't show up or respond to the lawsuit. For them it's all about easy money. Statistically speaking, only one in ten consumers who are sued over a debt even respond or show up in court. This is a very sad fact: consumers are giving up their legal right to force these firms to prove they owe a debt or the amount actually owed.

Whether you owe a debt or not, this book will give you the tools that you can use to get these lawyers off your back. An attorney friend of mine once told me, "This is America: deny everything and make them prove you owe them, if they can't you win". In as many as ninety percent (90%) of credit card debt lawsuits, the lawyers filing the suits don't have the documentation to prove that you owe the debt and I'll show you how and what to file in court to make them back off.

It is my recommendation to retain legal counsel if you can afford it; if you are unable to, this book will give you the tools to fight back.

I sincerely hope the information provided in the following chapters will help you beat the debt collectors just as I have.

STICK IT TO SUE HAPPY DEBT COLLECTORS

REMEMBER: Credit card lawsuits are civil lawsuits. They CANNOT put you in jail even if you lose. So if you are worried or scared, DON'T BE. Most of these sorts of lawsuits are scare tactics used by debt collectors and debt collection law firms; their hope is to frighten you enough that you won't answer or respond. When they see that you are fighting back and they must work for the money, often times they'll go away.

CREDIT CARD DEBT LAWSUITS ARE SCARE TACTICS.

Contents

I	Important Things You May Not Know About Debt Lawsuits	1
II	Defending Yourself (Pro Se) Is Mostly Paperwork	5
III	Original Creditor Lawsuits	8
IV	Debt Buyer (Junk Debt Collectors) Lawsuits	88
V	Dealing with Debt Collectors Before They Sue You	148
	DISCLAIMER	

THINGS YOU MAY NOT KNOW ABOUT DEBT LAWSUITS

Did you know that roughly eighty percent (80%) of credit cards are owned by just twelve (12) large banks? Unfortunately, it's true.

Did you know that nearly all credit cards receivables (balances owed by consumers and businesses) are sold by banks as asset backed securities and governed by the Security and Exchange Commission (SEC)? The reason why I am telling you this is that you can use this in court when sued. I will explain more about this in Chapter 3 - Original Creditor Lawsuits.

Did you know in upwards of ninety-percent (90%) of credit card debt lawsuits that are filed; the opposing attorney has insufficient proof that you owe the debt? The reason is that the proper documentation was either lost or never transferred to the law firm or the debt buyer.

Did you know that many times a debt collection law firm will pull your credit report and that this practice is against the law? Often a debt collection law firm will pull your credit report to see if you are worth suing. I call this a "lawsuit fishing expedition". It's also illegal. The Fair Credit Reporting Act (FCRA) specifically states that litigation is not permissible use of a consumer's credit report as it does not involve a business to consumer transaction. You can sue them for this. Be sure to read Chapter 5 - Dealing with Debt Collectors Before They Sue You, as I will go into more detail about it there.

Did you know that most debt collection law firms are actually third parties to original creditor lawsuits and have committed fraud upon the court when they filed the lawsuit? In most cases the original creditor has assigned the collection of a debt to a debt collection company, which in turn will assign the debt to a law firm in order to file suit and attempt to be awarded a judgment against you. While sometimes this is hard to prove in the beginning, there are several ways to prove that the law firm is

THINGS YOU MAY NOT KNOW ABOUT DEBT LAWSUITS

actually a third party. If we can prove that, then anything the attorney(s) submit as evidence (or via affidavit) is pure hearsay and cannot be used as evidence in court. I will cover how to find this out in Chapter 3 and in Chapter 4.

Did you know that one in ten (1 in 10) consumers served with a debt lawsuit will never respond or show up (for whatever reason). In some cases, the consumer was never made aware of the lawsuit or possibly, it could be because of embarrassment or fear.

Did you know that most of what it takes to defend yourself in court is the paperwork to be filed? It's true. Let's face it, for most of us, our eyes glaze over when they hear words like interrogatories, affidavits, affirmative defenses. I am going to break everything down so that even a young child could understand. These "big" words have very simple meanings. I will explain everything in plain and easy terms so that you will understand how to use them in court. I will show you what and how to file answers, motions to dismiss, sworn denials, etc.

STICK IT TO SUE HAPPY DEBT COLLECTORS

Did you know that debt lawsuits are civil lawsuits and you can't be put in jail if you lose? That's right; you can't be put in jail even if you lose the lawsuit. Most debt lawsuits never get past the "paperwork" stage. I am going to show you how to capitalize on that and get those lawyers off your back quickly.

IF I CAN REPRESENT MYSELF IN COURT AND WIN, SO CAN YOU. SO LET'S GET STARTED!

DEFENDING YOURSELF (PRO SE) IS MOSTLY PAPERWORK

Most debt lawsuits never make it to trial. Many never get past what I call the "paperwork stage". The paperwork stage is the beginning of the lawsuit and begins after you are served via a summons and complaint. The first step will be to file your Answer and Affirmative defenses. Soon as the answer is filed, you'll file a Motion to Dismiss. These two things alone will give even the most seasoned attorney a fit. In most cases after the plaintiff's attorney receives the Motion to Dismiss that you will file, he'll give up and file a voluntary dismissal.

My goal when responding to either an original creditor or junk debt buyer lawsuits is to overwhelm the opposing attorney and forcing the burden of proof on them. As I said earlier, debt collection attorneys and law firms are looking for easy money. I turn the tables and force them to work hard for a judgment.

Most of the debt collector/law firm attorneys are not going to spend much time or money proving a case; they would prefer to be awarded a default judgment. Time is money to them, and you can bet if they see that it is going to involve a lot of both, they'll roll over and go away.

At first glance representing yourself in court (*Pro Se*) appears to be complicated and overwhelming. In reality it is anything but, it's mostly paperwork that is filed in the court clerk's office. Chances are you may never even see the judge presiding over the complaint.

There are complete areas of study regarding the history of legal language including Latin and early English, the creation of laws, administrative acts, and even legalese used in private negotiations. For many it all might as well be Mandarin Chinese! It's used in virtually every case though, and I will explain each as we go along.

In both original creditor (Chapter 3) and debt buyer (Chapter 4) lawsuits we will cover: How to Answer a complaint, Affirmative

DEFENDING YOURSELF (PRO SE) IS MOSTLY PAPERWORK

Defenses, Motions to Dismiss, How to File a Sworn Denial, Interrogatories, Requests for Production of Documents and Requests for Admission. I will explain each and give examples on how to use them. As I have said previously most of defending yourself in court it just paperwork.

ORIGINAL CREDITOR LAWSUITS

An Original Creditor lawsuit is one that is brought by the company that originally granted you credit, such as a credit card company, bank, or other lender. There is a bit of a difference in how to defend an original creditor lawsuit versus defending a debt buyer (junk debt collections) lawsuit. In most cases, an original creditor civil lawsuit will name the creditor as plaintiff and the civil action will be titled "Suit on Account" or something similar in the complaint.

Credit card "Suit on Account" civil lawsuits are a bit dangerous for consumers. If a judgment is granted without being challenged, then the attorneys don't have to prove what you really owe in regard to actual charges or interest rates. We *MUST* make them prove everything. The more *Pro Se* consumers that do will eventually slow down or perhaps stop these kinds of lawsuits altogether.

Below are the basics and examples of how I implemented each item when defending myself. In most cases, you will need to do a bit of research to find proper legal citations and decisions. Please note that you can use legal precedence (legal decisions) even though they are not from your state. Debt collection attorneys do it all the time in civil actions and response filings. However, you should attempt to use laws and legal precedents from your state when possible: the more you use the better. I live in the State of Georgia and most states are similar in law.

First of all, when you are served a summons by a debt collection law firm you must respond or risk them being awarded a default judgment against you. Default judgments are easy money for the law firms, as they don't have to do anything other than file for a judgment for you failing to respond. If awarded a default judgment, then they can, most likely garnish your wages, bank accounts, etc.

Defendants that respond and show up in court win ninety percent (90%) of the lawsuits filed against them.

Answering the Complaint and Affirmative Defenses – Deny Everything

A very prominent consumer protection attorney once told me that when filing an answer to a summons, I should deny everything. Meaning, that I should force them to prove I owe the money, that's what the courts are for.

After I answer a complaint, I file a Motion to Dismiss and a Sworn Denial (a graduated denial). It is extremely important to file what is called a graduated denial. I will explain what a graduated denial is and how to file one later in this chapter.

Many times the original creditor has assigned the debt out to a debt collection company, which in turn re-assigns it to a debt collection law firm. Chances are very high that the law firm filing suit is actually a third party to the suit, meaning everything they enter into evidence is hearsay and possibly committed fraud on the court by filing the complaint to begin with. Very rarely does a credit card company send the debt for collection directly to a law firm. I will explain in further detail later.

I received a summons and complaint from an attorney some time ago. It was a civil "Suit on Account" lawsuit, with a one-page boilerplate agreement attached. I denied everything except the portion of the complaint that had my name and where I lived.

Below is an example only and any use of the information needs to be put on a legal filing form, sometimes called a Pleading Form. See your local court for example or use the same outline as the original complaint. All filings *must* to be notarized and filed in a timely manner. I also include "verification" and a "Certificate of Service" (proof that the plaintiff's attorney was sent a copy).

Example Answer and Affirmative Defenses

This is how I answered the "Suit on Account" complaint. When answering a complaint you have only three options: *True* (admitted as true), *Denied* (denied as untrue), or *"neither admitted true or denied because I do not enough information to know the truth of the matter"*. In my answer, I denied everything to do with the debt in question and only admitted as true the allegation that contained my name, street address and the state I live in. This is the beginning of forcing the plaintiff's attorneys to prove that I owe a debt. After I answered the complaint I list the affirmative defenses as to why I answered the way I did. This also sets in place what I will use in motions to dismiss and other filings. It tells the filing attorney to get ready as I plan on attacking the lawsuit.

At the end of the example, I have listed other affirmative defenses that may apply to you in addition to those that I have used, so be sure to read them as well.

I have explained each affirmative defense I used after the example.

ANSWER TO COMPLAINT ON ACCOUNT

My name is XXXXX XXXXXXXXXXX, and I am representing myself in this action. In response to each of the numbered paragraphs of the Plaintiff's Complaint or Petition, I state as follows:

1. The allegations of Paragraph One are: True (this is the line that had my name and place of residence on it)

2. The allegations of Paragraph Two are: Denied

3. The allegations of Paragraph Three are: Denied

4. The allegations of Paragraph Four are: Denied

AFFIRMATIVE DEFENSES

1. The Complaint fails to state a claim upon which relief may be granted.

2. Plaintiff's claims are barred by the doctrine of laches.

(#3 pertains to the state of Georgia only and varies from state to state.)

3. Plaintiff's claims are barred by the statute of frauds, O.C.G.A. § 13-5-30 as the purported contract or agreement falls within a class of contracts or agreements that are required to be in writing. The purported contract alleged in the Complaint was not in writing and not signed by Defendant or by some another person authorized by Defendant and who was to answer to the alleged debt, default, or miscarriage of the other person.

4. Plaintiff's claims are barred by the principle of waiver.

5. Plaintiff's claims are based on a contract that is an adhesion contract, and as such, all or portions of it are unenforceable.

6. Plaintiff's claims are based on a contract that is illusory and therefore unenforceable.

7. Plaintiff's calculation of interest is usurious or based on a rate that is greater than allowed by law.

8. Plaintiff has failed to state a valid claim for attorney fees, and is barred from collecting Attorney fees under the Fair Debt Collection Practices Act.

9. Plaintiff is barred under the Fair Debt Collection Practices Act, from collecting attorney fees, interest, collection fees, and any amount not specifically provided for by purported agreement.

10. Plaintiff's counsel did not afford Defendant due process of the law.

11. If allowed by this court the defendant reserves the right to plead other affirmative defenses that may become available at a later time.

Date
Signed

[NOTARY PUBLIC]

ORIGINAL CREDITOR LAWSUITS

Explanations of the Affirmative Defenses

1. Claim for Relief – The attorney did not attach proper evidence or claim to the complaint, just the boiler plate agreement (which may or may not be the proper one and did not additional amended terms of the agreement). They cannot prove any set of facts in support of their claim, which would entitle them to relief.
2. Barred by the Doctrine of Laches - Doctrine of Laches limits the legal claim of a person, by virtue of any undue delay on his part in enforcing his legal right. (Remember they only attached a single boilerplate agreement and they improperly filed a Suit on Account instead of a Breach of Contract).
3. Barred by the Statute of Frauds – This is a requirement that certain contracts (such as for sale of land, sale of goods exceeding a certain value, a debt guaranty) must be in writing and properly executed to prevent fraud and perjury. Otherwise such contracts cannot be enforced in the courts although they remain legal (are not rendered void). The statute of frauds varies from state to state.
4. Principle of Waiver - According to Black's Law Dictionary, the equitable principle of waiver is defined as "the intentional or voluntary relinquishment of a known right," a "renunciation, repudiation, abandonment, or surrender of some claim, right, privilege, or of the opportunity to take advantage of some defect, irregularity, or wrong."
5. Contract that is an Adhesion Contract - A contract of adhesion is a standard form contract, prepared by one party and presented to the weaker party, usually a consumer who has

no bargaining power and little or no choice about its terms." BLACKS LAW DICTIONARY (7th Ed.) p.318. - Credit Card contracts of adhesion have been found unconscionable and unenforceable. Discover Bank v. Superior Court of Los Angeles Cal 4th 2005 Cal. LEXIS 6686.

6. Contract that is illusory and therefore unenforceable. (Remember they only attached the boilerplate agreement and not subsequent amended terms of the agreement, chances are they'll never be able to provide 100% of the agreement and amended terms, thus it doesn't in reality exist).
7. Calculation of interest is usurious – basically they jacked up the interest rate (universal default) and that the interest rate is way above legal limits. (With the enacted CARD Act of 2009 this is very important, as they may have broken the law).
8. Plaintiff has failed to state a valid claim for attorney fees, and is barred from collecting Attorney fees under the Fair Debt Collection Practices Act. – Pretty much self-explanatory.
9. Plaintiff is barred under the Fair Debt Collection Practices Act – This may or may not float as the plaintiff is supposedly the original creditor (unless it was never transferred back to them form the Asset Backed Securities).
10. Plaintiff's counsel did not afford Defendant due process of the law – In my case I sent request for debt validation via certified mail, under the FDCPA they should have stopped collection efforts until such time that they provided the validation (proof) of the debt.

11. This one leaves the door open for me to file more defenses should the need arise.

Other Affirmative Defenses

These additional affirmative defenses may apply to you in original credit lawsuits.

Plaintiff's Complaint is time-barred Pursuant to [YOUR STATES STATUTE OF LIMITATIONS CODE HERE]

Every state has a statute of limitations on how long a person can wait to sue over a debt. You will need to check your state laws regarding statute of limitations. You can either search via a search engine or look it up at the local library in their law section.

Defendant claims Lack of Privity, as Defendant has never entered into any contractual or debtor/creditor arrangements with Plaintiff.

The doctrine of privity in contract law provides that a contract cannot confer rights or impose obligations arising under it on any person or agent except the parties to it. Only parties to contracts should be able to sue to enforce their rights or claim damages as such.

STICK IT TO SUE HAPPY DEBT COLLECTORS

The doctrine of privity can be problematic because implications upon contracts made for the benefit of third parties who are unable to enforce the obligations of the contracting parties.

The Plaintiff has not proven that they are authorized and licensed to collect claims for others in the State of [YOUR STATE], solicit the right to collect or receive payment of a claim of another.

You will need to check with your state laws to see if debt collectors have to be licensed and/or bonded to do business as a debt collector. Many states do not require debt collectors be licensed and/or bonded. This affirmative defense only applies to states that do.

The Complaint fails to allege or prove that the Plaintiff is licensed and has procured a bond in the State of YOUR STATE as required.

Again this only applies to states that require debt collectors to be licensed and/or bonded. This affirmative defense only applies to states that do.

Filing a Motion to Dismiss and Sworn Denials

You must answer the summons in order to file a Motion to Dismiss and a sworn denial. What I am about to lay out for you that has an excellent chance of the plaintiff's attorney voluntarily dismissing the lawsuit.

In many states (Georgia for one) credit card agreements whether expressed or implied have been ruled as being simple contracts, this is good thing from a consumer's standpoint. This means the action the Plaintiff's attorney filed is improper, as it should have been filed as a "Breach of Contract" not a "Suit on Account". (State of Georgia Decision) *Hill v. American Express 289 Ga. 576 657 S.E. 2nd 547.* This varies from state to state so you will have to do research of your states laws in order to find the particulars that fit your Motion to Dismiss.

In the case of the State of Georgia law you can access them via Lexis Nexis for free (this may apply to other states as well).

http://www.lexis-nexis.com/hottopics/gacode/default.asp

Many public libraries have a law section where you can research state law, local law and find your courts Rules of Civil Procedure. Many courts have a website that will have links to the courts Rules of Procedure. Most courts local rules mirror the states rules of civil procedure, but may list filing requirements such as a time frame for answers, motions, affidavits, etc. that are in addition to the states rules of Civil Procedure. So be sure to search for "[YOUR STATE] [COURT NAME] Rules" as well as "[YOUR STATE] Rules of Civil Procedure" and read through both.

From what I have found through my research is that all credit card companies bundle receivables (balances owed by consumers and businesses) and transfer them (and ownership) to a holding company, and then subsequently transfer these receivables to an asset backed securities fund and these are sold as securities to investors. When a receivable (credit card account) becomes delinquent (not paid) it is transferred back to the holding company. However, in many cases it is not clear if the delinquent receivable has ever been transferred back to the originator (credit card company).

If this is the case, then the attorney filed a civil suit naming an improper plaintiff. In order to sue someone on a debt you must be the owner of the debt. I use the search function at the US Security and Exchange Commission (SEC) website at www.sec.gov and search for the company (Capital One, American Express, Citibank, etc) and then look through the filings for "Asset Backed Securities".

Once you find an Asset Back Security offering for a particular company that fits the time frame(s) of when you had their credit card you will need to scroll through the securities form filing and find the filing titled "**Prospectus**". Every asset back security has one and it outlines how the fund operates. Most are quite long, however you can search for "delinquent" and/or "Default" to find out how the fund(s) transfers the receivables in the even an account becomes delinquent or defaulted.

At the time of this book being published, many of the Prospectus' do not clearly disclose how or to whom the account is transferred back to. They do not show that the account is transferred to the original creditor. That being the case then the original creditor cannot bring suit as they don't legally own the debt.

No matter the case, when used in a Motion to Dismiss, the plaintiff's attorney must respond and prove otherwise.

STICK IT TO SUE HAPPY DEBT COLLECTORS

The example below is what I have used on several occasions to secure a dismissal or better yet force an attorney to voluntarily dismiss a lawsuit.

Capital One Bank Credit Card Example

(Remember I found the asset backed securities information on the Securities and Exchange Commission, (www.sec.gov) website which is publically available to anyone.)

Since the credit card account in question was allegedly opened in 2005, I used a Prospectus from 2005.

Exhibit – S.E.C. Prospectus dated February 24, 2005 issued by Capital One Multi-Asset Execution Trust ("COMET") Form 424B5 – SEC Accession No. 0001193125-05-035704

Credit card issuers employ securitization schemes to raise capital for their operations. Capital One has employed and maintained the Capital One Master Trust Asset Backed Securities since July 1996.

The prospectus describes the securitization process used by Capital One Bank (USA) N.A., Plaintiff, Capital One Multi-Asset

ORIGINAL CREDITOR LAWSUITS

Execution Trust (COMET) and an entity called Capital One Funding, LLC.

As part of the process, ownership of selected accounts originated by the Plaintiff, Capital One Bank is transferred to Capital One Funding, LLC and then in turn transferred to COMET.

COMET then issues various classes of securities backed by the value of those accounts.

The master trust agreement provides Capital One Bank will service the accounts in exchange for a servicing fee. When an account goes into default and is charged off as uncollectible, it is automatically transferred from COMET back to Capital One Funding, LLC. It is not clear from the prospectus whether charged off accounts are ever transferred back to Capital One Bank.

As of March 31, 2008 COMET held almost 27 million consumer and business receivables representing over 43 billion dollars worth of receivables.

Given these numbers, there is a significant possibility that this particular account has gone through the securitization process and is no longer owned by Capital One Bank.

In many credit card debt lawsuits, the filing attorney will attach a boilerplate agreement to complaint as "evidence". The problem with the boilerplate agreement being attached is that it doesn't show all of the amended agreements of your credit card account and many times aren't the correct agreement for the credit card account. Sometimes the attorney will attach a credit card statement, this is not evidence but merely a partial listing of items purchased. When I see a single page of an agreement or one statement, I always assume that it's all the attorney has in regards to documentation, which will not hold up in court when I challenge it, and you can bet I do.

In my last case the Plaintiff's attorney attached a single page photocopy of a Capital One credit card agreement to the complaint and summons. The attorney did not include the full agreement or any of the amended terms of the original agreement. Basically this "evidence" is insufficient and in my Motion to Dismiss I use the Federal Truth in Lending Act to show that a single page of a card agreement is not the full agreement.

Example

Plaintiff has attached a credit card agreement to the complaint that has a machine typed copyright date of "xxxx" and a handwritten "x-x-xxxx to x-xx-xxxx" notation. The customer agreement attached to this Suit on Account is not the agreement in effect when this account was opened nor have any amended card agreements that pertain to this class of account have been attached.

A variety of interest rates and fees may have been applied to this account over its lifetime. The attached agreement does not specify the interest rate charged or the fee charges. These documents were issued separately from the agreement as is the custom of card issuers. These documents have not been attached.

A Plaintiff cannot recover interest or fees absent proof of an agreement to pay interest or fees.

Using the Federal Truth In Lending Act to Your Advantage

The Federal Truth in Lending Act requires material terms of a credit card relationship to set forth in a written agreement. Federal Law mandates comprehensive disclosures of these terms when the account is opened and when the account is amended. The precise content and format of the disclosures that must be made in connection with every credit card application is dictated in great detail by 1607 of the Act and the implementing regulation found at 12 C.F.R. 225.5 the basic terms for which disclo-disclosure is required includes:

- The annual percentage (%) rate applicable to the purchase, cash advances and balance transfers made using the account.
- The manner in which variable rates are determined.
- The amounts of annual fees or other fees for the issuance or availability of the card.
- The amounts of minimum finance charges and transaction charges.
- The existence and duration of a grace period, if any.
- The name of the balance calculation method and the amount of cash advance fees, late payment fees, over the limit fees and balance transfer fees 12 C.F.R. 225.5a(b)

The Act defined the manner and timing of such disclosures regardless of the manner in which the credit card offer is made, whether it is made by mail, telephone, in a catalog, magazine or other publication or over the internet. 15 U.S.C. § 1637(c) (1)-(7).

Additional disclosures are required in monthly statements, 12 C.F.R. 226.7, when the terms of the agreement are changed, 12 C.F.R. 226.9 (c) and before the card renewal date, 12 C.F.R. 226.9 (e).

Because these disclosures are required to be in writing and integrated into the account opening process regardless of how the account is opened, the disclosed terms become defacto terms of the card agreement.

Title 15 U.S.C. § 1642 (Issuance of Credit Cards) prohibits the gratuitous issuance of a credit card. Credit card is to be issued only in response to an application or request. Any such application or request is governed by the disclosure provisions of Title 15 U.S.C § 1637 (Open-end consumer credit plans).

It is impossible to lawfully establish a credit card account without a comprehensive written document setting forth virtually all of the material terms of the agreement.

Allowing the Plaintiff to sue on account stated theory to imply an agreement to pay interest and fees stated relieves him from establishing the amount of interest and fees that were disclosed under Federal Law and that were included in the terms of its express agreement, permitting Plaintiff an unjustified windfall or unjust enrichment.

Breach of Contract Not Suit on Account

If your state upholds credit card agreements as simple contracts then the attorney improperly filed the civil action. It should have been filed as a "Breach of Contract" rather than a "Suit on Account".

This is how I dealt with the "Suit on Account" claim.

Plaintiff is suing as Suit On Account. The elements of the account stated cause of action expressly draw a distinction between suits that grow out of course of dealing and suits that grow out of an express agreement. Cental Ntl Bank of San Angelo v. Cox 96, S.W. 2nd 746,748. The court said:

- The cases are legion on what constitutes an account stated. In general the essential elements are: Transactions between the parties, which give rise to an

indebtedness of one to the other; an agreement expressed or implied, between them fixing the amount due: and a promise, express or implied, by the one to be charged, to pay such indebtedness.
- The first and defining element of the claim is the existence of a debtor-creditor relationship that arises from a series of transactions – from a course of dealing, not a contract. This element is identical across all suits on account, whether open, sworn, or stated.

An account stated theory may have been appropriate when credit card issuers gave card holders fixed interest rates and charged very few fees. With the proliferation of credit cards over the last two decades, however interest rates have varied and fees have increased in number and severity.

This suit only lists indebtedness in the amount $X,XXX.XX principal, and interest of $X,XXX.XX which works out to a simple interest rate of XX.X%. There is no notation of fees. A detailed account of the charges, interest and fees are required as Plaintiff cannot recover interest or fees absent proof of an agreement to pay interest or fees. Statements are evidence of interest rate that was actually charged NOT the rate that the parties agreed to. Tully v. Citibank (South Dakota) N.A. 173 S.W 3d 212,216 2005 and Hay v. Citibank (South Dakota) N.A.,

STICK IT TO SUE HAPPY DEBT COLLECTORS

2006 WL 2620089. Absent proof of agreed upon rate, Plaintiff should not be awarded damages based upon failure to pay the rates demanded in the monthly statements.

At this point, what I have written may not make a lot of sense so please bear with me as I explain. The Motion to Dismiss and Sworn Denial are the keys to forcing the attorney to back off. When you file a Motion to Dismiss, the filing attorney has so many days (varies from state to state) in which to respond to the motion. Once they read the motion with all that I am sharing with you, they will most likely file a voluntary dismissal, or they may not even respond to the motion. If they don't respond there is a very good chance the judge will grant your dismissal.

There is a very good chance the judge will grant the motion anyway regardless of the attorney's response. If the attorney does not respond at all, again the judge may grant your Motion to Dismiss as it wasn't contested. Judges do not appreciate their courts time being tied up, or time wasted by idiot attorneys that do not respond properly (this is a good thing for you).

If by chance they do respond to the Motion to Dismiss and the judge grants their denial we still have a trick up our collective sleeves to force them to produce the documentation, answer questions and admit whether or not they have certain things (such as the original agreement). These are called "Discovery Request for Production of Documents, Interrogatories (questions that must be answered) and Request for Admissions". I will explain each in further detail later in this chapter.

The Motion to Dismiss and Sworn Denial Bombshell
In order to make any affidavits filed by the Plaintiffs attorney worthless from a legal standpoint I file what is called a Sworn Denial. I file it in such a way that it is not an outright denial, but a *gradual denial* (see example below). Once I file this with the court clerk's office, any affidavit filed by the Plaintiffs attorney becomes hearsay and cannot be used as evidence in court. You will need to file this in the same format and have it notarized the same manner as you did would the Answer and Motion to Dismiss.

I file both a Sworn Denial and a Motion to Dismiss at the same time. I want both to be in effect at the same time because I reference the Sworn Denial in my Motion to Dismiss.

SWORN DENIAL

I deny that this is my debt and if it is my debt, I deny that it is still a valid debt and if it is a valid debt, I deny the amount sued for in the amount of $X,XXX.XX principal, $X,XXX.XX as interest including attorney fees is the correct amount.

DATE

Signed

[NOTARY PUBLIC]

MOTION TO DISMISS

As you will see below most of what I wrote about earlier is included. Some of the items may or may not pertain to you (unless you live in the State of Georgia). The example below is one I filed in a Capital One lawsuit Motion to Dismiss, you will need to search and replace proper verbiage in the motion to fit your needs.

Several items below may not pertain to your particular motion, if they don't then do not use them. Motions to Dismiss should be simple, clear and to the point.

MOTION TO DISMISS

MEMORANDUM OF POINTS AND AUTHORITIES

Comes now the Defendant (FULL NAME), and files this Request for Dismissal of Complaint, as follows:

1. The Causes of Action specified in the complaint filed by the Plaintiff is insufficient as a matter of law.

The complaint does not set forth the True facts upon which Plaintiff seeks a summary judgment. The complaint should be dismissed.

2. Defendant received the Plaintiff's Complaint on or about XXXXXXXXX XX, 200X. Defendant answered the complaint on or about XXXXXXXXXXX X, 200X.

3. Defendant on or about XXXX XX, 200X requested in writing to Plaintiff's counsel to show proof of debt (debt validation request). To date neither Plaintiff nor counsel has responded to Defendant's request to show proof of debt.

4. IMPROPER PLAINTIFF

Exhibit – S.E.C. Prospectus dated February 24, 2005 issued by Capital One Multi-Asset Execution Trust ("COMET") Form 424B5 – SEC Accession No. 0001193125-05-035704

Credit card issuers employ securitization schemes to raise capital for their operations. Capital One has employed and maintained the Capital One Master Trust Asset Backed Securities since July 1996.

ORIGINAL CREDITOR LAWSUITS

The prospectus describes the securitization process used by Capital One Bank (USA) N.A., Plaintiff, Capital One Multi-Asset Execution Trust (COMET) and an entity called Capital One Funding, LLC.

As part of the process, ownership of selected accounts originated by the Plaintiff, Capital One Bank is transferred to Capital One Funding, LLC and then in turn transferred to COMET.

COMET then issues various classes of securities backed by the value of those accounts.

The master trust agreement provides Capital One Bank will service the accounts in exchange for a servicing fee. When an account goes into default and is charged off as uncollectible, it is automatically transferred from COMET back to Capital One Funding, LLC. It is not clear from the prospectus whether charged off accounts are ever transferred back to Capital One Bank.

As of March 31, 2008 COMET held almost 27 million consumer and business receivables representing over 43 billion dollars worth of receivables.

Given these numbers, there is a significant possibility that this particular account has gone through the securitization process and is no longer owned by Capital One Bank.

5. Plaintiff has not proved or established that I am the person who applied for or used this credit card. Defendant has issued a Sworn Denial in this matter. First requisite element of debt is the existence of obligation. Ernst v. Jessie L. Riddle PC, MD La 1997.

Davis v. Discover Bank, 277 Ga. App. 864
Davis did not deny use of card but that Davis did not sign a contract.

6. Plaintiff has attached a credit card agreement to the complaint that has a machine typed copyright date of 2005 and a handwritten 4-1-2005 to 6-30-2008 notation. The customer agreement attached to this Suit on Account is not the agreement in effect when this account was opened nor have any amended card agreements that pertain to this class of account have been attached.

7. A variety of interest rates and fees may have been applied to this account over its lifetime. The attached agreement does not

specify the interest rate charged or the fee charges. These documents were issued separately from the agreement as is the custom of card issuers. These documents have not been attached.

8. Plaintiff cannot recover interest or fees absent proof of an agreement to pay interest or fees.

9. Plaintiff is suing as Suit On Account. The elements of the account stated cause of action expressly draw a distinction between suits that grow out of course of dealing and suits that grow out of an express agreement. Cental Ntl Bank of San Angelo v. Cox 96, S.W. 2nd 746,748. The court said:

- The cases are legion on what constitutes an account stated. In general the essential elements are: Transactions between the parties which give rise to an indebtedness of one to the other; an agreement expressed or implied, between them fixing the amount due: and a promise, express or implied, by the one to be charged, to pay such indebtedness.
- The first and defining element of the claim is the existence of a debtor-creditor relationship that arises from a series of transactions – from a course of dealing, not a contract. This element is identical across all suits on account, whether open, sworn or stated.

STICK IT TO SUE HAPPY DEBT COLLECTORS

An account stated theory may have been appropriate when credit card issuers gave card holders fixed interest rates and charged very few fees. With the proliferation of credit cards over the last two decades however, interest rates have varied and fees have increased in number and severity.

This suit only lists indebtedness in the amount $X,XXX.XX principal, and interest of $X,XXX.XX which works out to a simple interest rate of XX.X%. There is no notation of fees. A detailed account of the charges, interest and fees are required as Plaintiff cannot recover interest or fees absent proof of an agreement to pay interest or fees. Statements are evidence of interest rate that was actually charged NOT the rate that the parties agreed to. Tully v. Citibank (South Dakota) N.A. 173 S.W 3d 212,216 2005 and Hay v. Citibank (South Dakota) N.A., 2006 WL 2620089. Absent proof of agreed upon rate, Plaintiff should not be awarded damages based upon failure to pay the rates demanded in the monthly statements.

The Federal Truth in Lending Act requires material terms of a credit card relationship to set forth in a written agreement. Federal Law mandates comprehensive disclosures of these terms when the account is opened and when the account is amended.

ORIGINAL CREDITOR LAWSUITS

The precise content and format of the disclosures that must be made in connection with every credit card application is dictated in great detail by 1607 of the Act and the implementing regulation found at 12 C.F.R. 225.5. The basic terms for which disclosure is required include:

- The annual percentage (%) rate applicable to the purchase, cash advances and balance transfers made using the account.
- The manner in which variable rates are determined.
- The amounts of annual fees or other fees for the issuance or availability of the card.
- The amounts of minimum finance charges and transaction charges.
- The existence and duration of a grace period, if any.
- The name of the balance calculation method and the amount of cash advance fees, late payment fees, over the limit fees and balance transfer fees 12 C.F.R. 225.5a(b)

The Act defined the manner and timing of such disclosures regardless of the manner in which the credit card offer is made, whether it is made by mail, telephone, in a catalog, magazine or other publication or over the internet. 15 U.S.C. § 1637(c) (1)-(7).

Additional disclosures are required in monthly statements, 12 C.F.R. 226.7, when the terms of the agreement are changed, 12 C.F.R. 226.9 (c) and before the card renewal date, 12 C.F R. 226.9 (e).

Because these disclosures are required to be in writing and integrated into the account opening process regardless of how the account is opened, the disclosed terms become defacto terms of the card agreement.

Title 15 U.S.C. § 1642 (Issuance of Credit Cards) prohibits the gratuitous issuance of a credit card. A credit card is to be issued only in response to an application or request. Any such application or request is governed by the disclosure provisions of Title 15 U.S.C § 1637 (Open end consumer credit plans).

It is impossible to lawfully establish a credit card account without a comprehensive written document setting forth virtually all of the material terms of the agreement.

Allowing Plaintiff to sue on account stated theory to imply an agreement to pay interest and fees stated relieves him from establishing the amount of interest and fees that were disclosed under Federal Law and that were included in the terms of its express agreement, permitting Plaintiff an unjustified windfall or unjust enrichment.

10. Breach of Contract

Georgia Law has upheld that a credit card account is a simple contract. Hill v. American Express 289 Ga. 576 657 S.E. 2nd 547.

Plaintiff is limited to only what can be pleaded and proved under the written contract. Truly v. Austin, 744 S.W. 2nd. 934,936 (Tex 1988)

A schedule of the charges, interest and fees are required as Plaintiff cannot recover interest or fees absent proof of an agreement to pay interest or fees.

11. This is a contract of adhesion, "A contract of adhesion is a standard form contract, prepared by one party and presented to the weaker party, usually a consumer who has no bargaining power and little or no choice about its terms." BLACKS LAW DICTIONARY (7th Ed.) p. 318.

STICK IT TO SUE HAPPY DEBT COLLECTORS

Historically Georgia courts have held that in contracts of adhesion the party who has little to no control of the terms of the contract is to be favored.

12. Credit Card contracts of adhesion have been found unconscionable and unenforceable. Discover Bank v. Superior Court of Los Angeles Cal 4th 2005 Cal. LEXIS 6686.

Congress acknowledged the abuse of contract that allowed for Universal Default, interest rate changes at will and at will fee charges with the enacted Credit Card Reform Act (CARD Act) of 2009.

(#13 applies to the state of Georgia only)

13. A contract cannot be enforced if its terms are incomplete, vagur, indefiniter or uncertain. In addition the party asserting the existence of a contract has the burden of proving its existence and its term. This proof must be clear and convincing. Cumberland Center Assoc. v. Southeast Mgnt Ect Corp 228 Ga. App. 571-575 (1) 492 Se2d 546 (1997)

14. Plaintiff's Counsel [LAW FIRM NAME HERE] do not directly represent [PLAINTIFF NAME HERE] but represents a

second party and/or parties that represents the Plaintiff, thus all evidence must be treated as hearsay as [LAW FIRM NAME HERE] are third parties to the Suit on Account.

15. Plaintiffs' counsel committed fraud upon the court by filing the Suit on Account.

WHEREFORE, Defendant, [FULL NAME HERE], respectfully submits that the Court should dismiss and deny the Plaintiff's complaint, filed herein [PLAINTIFF NAME HERE] and prays for Dismissal of the complaint by the Plaintiff.

Defendant's Request submitted this XX day, of XXXXXXXX 200X.

_____

Defendant pro se

Address: Street address, City State, Zip
Telephone: (XXX) XXX-XXXX

[NOTARY PUBLIC]

(Along with this I included a verification and certificate of service)

Along with the Motion to Dismiss I also included a judge's order for dismissal (to make it easier for the judge, many times this is required in a Motion to Dismiss filing). *See the following page for example.*

ORDER FOR DISMISSAL

WHEREFORE, in consideration of Defendant's Motion for Dismissal, it is hereby ORDERED and ADJUCATED that Defendant's motion shall be granted.

SO ORDERED this _____ day of _____, 200X.

_____
JUDGE
[STATE OR COUNTY COURT and YOUR COUNTY]

Example Verification

VERIFICATION

Personally appeared before me the undersigned who on oath states that the facts set forth in this MOTION TO DISMISS are true and correct to the best of her knowledge and belief.

_____,

Defendant pro se

[NOTARY PUBLIC]

Example Certificate of Service

CERTIFICATE OF SERVICE

I hereby certify that I have this day served the foregoing MOTION TO DISMISS upon counsel for all parties, by depositing a copy of same in the United States mail in an envelope with sufficient postage thereon addressed as follows:

[ATTORNEY'S NAME and MAILING ADDRESS]

This XX day of XXXXX 200X.

_____

Defendant

Address: [Street address, city, state, zip]
Phone: (XXX) XXX-XXXXX

[NOTARY PUBLIC]

Remember that you must send a copy of the certificate of service and the Motion to Dismiss to the opposing attorney via certified mail. Be sure to have all copies of the motion, verification, and certificate of service time-stamped at the court clerk's office. Anything you file with the court clerk should be notarized, even original copies that you send to the opposing attorney. I also time-stamp and notarize my personal copies in case I have need for them in court at a later time.

In most cases after the opposing attorney reads through the Motion to Dismiss, he or she will see that you aren't playing games and that you are going to fight tooth and nail. If the Plaintiff's attorney knows they can't respond with proper documentation as you outlined in the Motion to Dismiss, he will most likely abandon the lawsuit by filing a voluntary dismissal. Debt collection attorneys prefer easy money they receive from default judgments; they will rarely work hard if they know they have an uphill battle ahead of them to prove their case. This is to your advantage when being sued.

In rare cases the Plaintiff attorney will attempt to respond to your Motion to Dismiss (most won't), if they do and the judge denies your motion then we'll file a couple of things and force the Plaintiffs attorney to produce documentation such as the original agreement and any amended agreement terms (remember the Truth In Lending Act), answer questions (Interrogatories) and to admit or deny facts in the case (Request for Admissions).

Motion to Strike Affidavit of Debt or Affidavit of Account

SEE CHAPTER 4 - Motion to Strike Affidavit of Debt or Affidavit of Account

Discovery - Interrogatories, Request for Production of Documents, Request for Admissions

While this varies from court to court, see your courts Rules of Civil Procedure (may also be called "Trial Rules") on when you can file motions or discovery requests (make them provide documents the Plaintiff has). Rules of Civil Procedure are generally a list of how the court and court system operates. It may tell you when you can file certain kinds of filings (like Motions to Dismiss, Discovery, etc). The Rules of Procedure may also include the timeframe in which parties have to answer motions and file responses. You can usually find the Rules of Procedure for a particular court using a search engine. Most courts websites have a link to their Rules of Procedure. In many cases, a state's Rules of Civil Procedure govern local courts. However, many local courts have additional court rules that must be abided by. Most of the time they are simple and easy to understand and further stipulate specific timeframes of when filing must be made.

The courts here, where all of the debt lawsuits have been filed against me, are bound by the State of Georgia's Rules for Civil Procedure. The Rules of Civil Procedure does not state any particular timeframe to file for Discovery. The only stipulation is that I must make request for Discovery within six months of my answering the complaint. In other words, I can file them at any time after I answer the summons and complaint. The only exception is that if I file a Motion to Dismiss there is an automatic stay of discovery for 90 days. I generally wait and see if the Plaintiff's attorney is going to respond to my Motion to Dismiss or file a voluntary dismissal. If they respond to my motion, I then I start planning my next angle of attack using Discovery requests such as Interrogatories, Request for Production of Documents, and Request for Admissions.

In most courts, the receiving attorney has a certain timeframe in which to respond to you your requests (usually 30 days). If they don't respond you can file what it called a "Motion to Compel". A motion to compel tells the court/judge that the other attorney is refusing to answer your questions and asks the court to force them to comply. To date I haven't had to file a motion to compel and have no example for you. I am sure there are quite a few examples available on the Internet and a quick search will find them.

In the event that the receiving attorney still doesn't respond in the timeframe allowed you can file a "Motion to Deem Admissions Admitted" with the court. If this is granted, and most likely will be if the opposing attorney doesn't respond, then, by default they are admitting that they don't have the documents requested in your discovery request. This means your entire discovery is admitted and this is not good for the opposing attorney. In other words, they have no case. To date I haven't had to file a motion to deem admissions admitted and have no example for you. I am sure there are quite a few examples available on the Internet and a quick search will find them.

If the opposing attorney fails to answer your requests for discovery, especially after a motion to compel is filed, you might decide to be vindictive and file a lawsuit against the law firm for filing a frivolous lawsuit. You may also want to file a complaint with your state's Bar Association against the filing attorney (he might be disbarred). You may even ask the judge to impose sanctions against the opposing attorney.

DISCOVERY

Discovery is a category of procedural devices (methods) employed by a party to a civil or criminal action, prior to trial, to require the adverse party to disclose information that is essential for the preparation of the requesting party's case and that the other party alone knows or possesses. Interrogatories, Requests for Production of Documents, and Requests for Admissions are all forms of discovery.

INTERROGATORIES

Interrogatories are nothing more than a series of written questions served upon the opposing party in order to discover certain facts regarding disputed issues. The answers to Interrogatories must be under oath and served within a prescribed period.

REQUEST FOR PRODUCTION OF DOCUMENTS

A request for the Production of Documents is a request to a party to surrender certain defined documents. Credit card agreements, amended agreement terms, assignments of debt, etc. are examples of documents that can be requested.

REQUEST FOR ADMISSIONS

A Request for Admissions is a request to a party that they admit certain facts. One party sends the other a Request for Admission so that basic issues the parties agree upon can be resolved and not have to be proven if the parties go to trial.

You need to check with your local courts or state rules of civil procedure in regards to when you can file for discovery and how long they have to answer.

Remember, that as with the Answer and Affirmative Defense, Motion to Dismiss, etc., the discovery requests should be on a Pleading form, filed with the court clerk (unless the Rules of

Procedure state otherwise), be notarized and served upon the opposing counsel via certified mail.

Note that the example is for the State of Georgia. Again, keep in mind, if you live in another state you will need to change the state law references to your own state's laws pertaining to each.

Example of Discovery

(Interrogatories, Request for Documents and Request for Admissions)

DEFENDANT'S FIRST SET OF INTERROGATORIES,
REQUESTS FOR ADMISSIONS AND
REQUEST FOR PRODUCTION OF DOCUMENTS

[YOUR NAME HERE], Defendant

The Defendant requests the following discovery of the Plaintiff, pursuant to Georgia Rules of Civil Procedure O.C.G.A. § 9-11-26. Plaintiff is directed to serve its verified answers, and to produce the requested documents in conformance with the above-cited rules, on or before thirty (30) days from the date certified below, to the Defendant's Residence [YOUR ADDRESS

STICK IT TO SUE HAPPY DEBT COLLECTORS

HERE]. In the event you become aware of or acquire in your possession, custody or control, of additional responsive documents, you are asked promptly to produce such additional documents for inspection and copying.

INSTRUCTIONS AND DEFINITIONS

1. For the purposes of these discovery requests, the following definitions apply:

A. "Defendant" means [YOUR FULL NAME]. The alleged original creditor is [ORIGINAL CREDITOR NAME HERE]; and the account means any alleged account related to the debt.

B. "Plaintiff" or "Plaintiffs" refer to [PLAINTIFFS NAME HERE] as well as any person in their agency or employ.

C. "Creditor" refers to as well as any person in their agency or employ.

D. "FDCPA" refers to the Fair Debt collection Practices act in its entirety.

E. "Document" as used herein means, original, copies of original, or copies of any records, minutes, notices, books, papers, contracts, memoranda, invoices, correspondence, notes, calendars, photographs, drawings, charts, graphs other writings, recording tapes, recording discs, mechanical or electronic information storage or recording elements (including any information stored on a computer), written and recorded telephone messages, and any other "documents". If a document has been prepared in several copies, or additional copies have been made that are not identical (or are no longer identical by reason of subsequent notation or other modification of any kind whatsoever, including without limitation notations on the backs of pages thereof) each non-identical copy is a separate document.

F. "And", "or", and "and/or" shall be construed as broadly as possible so that information otherwise within the scope of the request is not excluded.

G. "Statement" or "Statements" means the periodic monthly statement issued by the plaintiff

H. "Assignment Agreement" includes but is not limited to bills of sale, the actual purchase and assignment agreement document(s) including the terms and conditions of the sale, and the schedule of accounts included in sale. Assignment Agreements shall also mean the complete documentation of the chain of custody between the original creditor and plaintiff.

I. "Application" means the document or documents submitted to the original creditor for the purposes of acquiring the account.

J. "Person" includes natural persons, corporations, partnerships, associations, or any type of entity, and agents, servants, employees, and representatives thereof.

K. The "debt" means the alleged debt that is the subject of this lawsuit.

L. The term "identify", when used in reference to an individual person or business entity means to state the person's or entity's full name, and if applicable, present occupation or position, professional qualifications, employer, employees, present business address, and present and past business affiliations with or relationships to any of the parties in this action known.

M. When used in reference to a document, "identify" means to describe the type of document (e.g., "letter"), date, author and addressee, to state the location of the documents and the name, address and relationship to each party in this action of each and every person who has such document in his or her possession, custody or control.

N. "Attorney" means [ATTORNEY NAME HERE]. Or any other Indiana Licensed Attorney employed by [ATTORNEYS FIRM NAME HERE].

O. Remember that answering the interrogatories, you must furnish all requested information, not subject to valid objection, that is known by, possessed by, or available to you or your subsidiaries, employers, employees, managers, attorneys, consultants, agents, or representatives.

P. If you are unable to fully answer any of these interrogatories, please answer them to the fullest extent possible, specify the reasons for your inability to further answer and state whatever information, knowledge or belief that you have concerning the portion not fully answered.

Q. Each numbered subpart of a numbered interrogatory is to be considered a separate interrogatory for the purpose of objection. Thus, you must object separately to each subpart; and if you object to less than all of the subparts of a numbered interrogatory, answer the remaining subparts.

R. If any information called for in these interrogatories is withheld on the ground that such information is for any reason exempt from discovery, then:

1. State the ground or grounds for withholding such information;

2. Describe the type of information being withheld;

3. Identify all persons who have knowledge of the information being withheld;

4. Furnish such other information as may be required to enable the court to adjudicate the propriety of your refusal to furnish such information;

S. Please remember that you are under a duty to seasonably supplement your response to each questions directly addressed to the identity and locations of persons having knowledge of discoverable matters, and other information that may come to you in the future.

1. For persons, state the person's name, residence address, business address, telephone number, and the name of his/her employer;

2. For entities, state the name and address of its principal place of business, telephone number (if the person's entity's present address in known, please give his/her last known address);

3. For documents, state the author, addressee and recipient, date, a general description, a brief summary of its contents, the name and address of the custodian or the original, or best copy, any other descriptive information necessary in order to adequately describe it in a subpoena duces tecum or in a request or motion for its production; in lieu of such identification, you may attach a copy of each document to your answer to these interrogatories;

4. For oral communications, state exactly what was said, when, where, by whom, to whom, and who else was in hearing distance; and identify all documents that mention, relate to, or have any connection with each such communications.

5. Whenever appropriate in these discovery requests, the singular and plural forms of words shall be interpreted interchangeably so as to bring within the scope of these requests any matter which might otherwise be construed outside their scope.

6. Unless otherwise indicated, these discovery requests apply to the time period commencing when the Defendant allegedly opened the account, through the present;

7. Except as expressly provided in a particular discovery request, all of the terms utilized in these discovery requests shall have the meaning given to them in the Georgia Rules of Civil Procedure.

CLAIMS OF PRIVILEGE

If an objection to a request is based upon a claim of privilege or attorney work product, identify each document so withheld. With regard to all documents or portions of documents withheld on this basis, identify its creator; provide a brief description of the document, and state with particularity the basis of the claim of privilege, work product, or other ground of nondisclosure.

LOST OR DESTROYED DOCUMENTS

If any document requested has been lost, discarded, or destroyed, identify such document. State the type of document, its date, the approximate date it was lost, discarded, or destroyed, the reason it was lost, discarded or destroyed, a summary of its substance, and the identity of each person having knowledge of the contents thereof.

INTERROGATORY #1

Is [LAW FIRM NAME HERE] the direct collection assignee of [PLAINTIFF NAME HERE]? Or, is [LAW FIRM NAME HERE] an assignee of an assignee? If there are additional assignees, identify each assignee, their business address, and telephone number.

INTERROGATORY #2

Identify when the alleged account was originally opened by the defendant and was subsequently charged off by [PLAINTIFF NAME HERE].

INTERROGATORY #3

Identify the person or persons answering these interrogatories. Include their business address, business phone number, and title within the Plaintiff's Organization.

INTERROGATORY #4

Provide the following information for each person known to the Plaintiff who has knowledge of facts relevant to this case, including but not limited to all persons interviewed by you, by your counsel, or by any person cooperating with you in the this action, giving a brief description thereof, for each person you may call as a witness in this case.

1. Name, address, and telephone number.

2. Place of Employment

3. Relation to the Plaintiff

4. The subjects and substance of the testimony the witness will give; and whether the witness is to be tendered as an expert witness.

INTERROGATORY #5

Provide the following information.

1. Your Full Name

2. Your Full Business Name

3. Your Business Purpose (e.g. Creditor, Lender, Collection Agency, etc.)

4. Form of Business Organization (e.g. corporation, partnership, LLC, sole proprietorship, etc.)

INTERROGATORY #6

In regards to the contract or agreement alleged in this action, please state the following:

1. Full Terms of the Agreement:

2. Credit Limit Amount Financed in the Alleged Contract or Agreement:

3. Date and Monetary value of any valuable consideration received on the contract or agreement:

4. Date and Monetary value of any payments or credits alleged to be executed on the contract or agreement:

INTERROGATORY #7

Provide the following information for each person who has had any involvement in any manner in any efforts on your behalf to collect or attempt to collect any debt (s) purportedly owing by Defendant.

1. His/Her Position

2. His/Her work address, telephone numbers

3. Nature and purpose of his/her involvement.

INTERROGATORY #8

Identify the persons or entities, regarding any debt(s), which you have attempted to collect from Defendant, identify all documents related or relevant to your contractual agreement(s) (Servicing, Assignment(s), etc.), or other business relationships with said persons or entities.

INTERROGATORY #9

Plaintiff and Attorney. Please Identify each person who has had any contact or communication on your behalf regarding Defendant's purported debt(s), state when, how, where, and with whom said contact or communication occurred and in detail and with particularity the substance thereof.

INTERROGATORY #10

Attorney. Describe all collection activities, which you were authorized to perform for [PLAINTIFFS NAME HERE], and identify the terms of the agreement between [PLAINTIFFS NAME HERE] and you pursuant to which you sought to collect this account.

INTERROGATORY #11

Describe [PLAINTIFFS NAME HERE] procedure and policy with respect to the Maintenance, preservation, and destruction of documents, stating in your Answer whether any documents or things relating to any information Requested in these interrogatories, or related in any way to this lawsuit, have ever been destroyed or are no longer in your custody. For each such document, please identify the document, how, when and why each document was destroyed or otherwise left your control, the identity of any person who participated in any way in the destruction and/or action for destroying the document or to transfer it out of your control or custody; and if the document still exists, identify the person now having control or custody of the document.

INTERROGATORY #12

What document states in writing in support of your Complaint that the Defendant is indebted to pay Plaintiff and when was this agreed statement in writing entered into?

INTERROGATORY #13

On what date did the defendant become indebted to the plaintiff for $[AMOUNT CLAIMED IN SUIT] plus accrued interest of $[INTEREST AMOUNT CLAIMED IN SUIT)?

INTERROGATORY #14

Identify all witnesses with evidence in support of your Complaint that the Defendant, entered into a contract and is indebted to the Plaintiff.

INTERROGATORY #15

State all actions taken to verify the accuracy and completeness of the accounts reported and state your procedures designed to assure the maximum possible accuracy of the information reported by you.

INTERROGATORY #16

What is the date that the defendant allegedly defaulted on the original account?

INTERROGATORY #17

What was the status of the alleged contract/account when collection assignment was made to [ATTORNEY FIRM NAME HERE]?

INTERROGATORY #18

What credit card purchases and/or cash advances were made on this account? When where they made?

INTERROGATORY #19

Please identify and describe each exhibit you will use in the trial of civil action: [CIVIL ACTION NUMBER HERE]:

INTERROGATORY #20

State fully, completely and at length the factual basis of each defense which you now assert or intend to assert in this action.

INTERROGATORY #21

As to each defense set out in response to Interrogatory Twenty (20), above, state the following as to notification to Defendant of such defenses; (a) the date or dates when notification was given; (b) the manner in which notification was given; and (c) the specific party or parties to whom notification was given.

INTERROGATORY #22

Do you have the Actual Original Contract or Agreement between the Defendant and [PLAINTIFFS NAME HERE]? And do you have the Original Collections Assignment Agreement between [PLAINTIFFS NAME HERE] and [LAW FIRM NAME HERE]?

REQUESTS FOR ADMISSIONS

The Defendant requests that the Plaintiff answer the following requests for Admissions pursuant to, and in accordance with, Georgia Rules of Civil Procedure O.C.G.A. § 9-11-36. If the Plaintiff objects to any requested admission, the reason therefore shall be stated. The Plaintiff's answer shall specifically admit or deny the requested admission, or set forth in detail the reasons why the Plaintiff cannot truthfully admit or deny the requested admission. A denial shall fairly meet the substance of the requested admission, and when good faith requires that the Plaintiff qualify an answer or deny only in part of the matter of which an admission is requested, the Plaintiff shall specify so much of it as is true and qualify or deny the remainder, again detailing the specificity of the denial of the part thereof.

ADMISSION #1

Admit that you were not assigned [PLANTIFFS NAME HERE] obligations under the assignment agreement.

ADMISSION #2

Admit that you do not have the original or a copy of an assignment between you and [PLAINTIFF NAME HERE].

ADMISSION #3

Admit that there was no written agreement, signed by Defendant, between Defendant and [PLAINTIFFS NAME HERE].

ADMISSION #4

Admit that there is no written agreement between [PLAINTIFFS NAME HERE] and the Defendant.

ADMISSION #5

Admit that you did not send the defendant any notification of assignment of the account or assignment of rights.

ADMISSION #6

Admit that as of the date you drafted your Complaint, you had no evidence admissible at trial that proves Defendant owes the debt.

ADMISSION #7

Admit that [LAW FIRM NAME HERE] are considered Debt collectors under the Fair Debt Collection Practices Act.

ADMISSION #8

Admit that you are barred under the Fair Debt Collection Practices Act § 1692 f(1) from collecting interest on any amount not authorized by the agreement creating the debt or permitted by law.

ADMISSION #9

ORIGINAL CREDITOR LAWSUITS

Admit that you do not have the agreement to claim the amount(s) submitted in the complaint.

ADMISSION #10

Admit that you do not have a copy of or the original [PLAINTIFF NAME HERE] Cardholder Agreement.

ADMISSION #11

Admit that [PLAINTIFFS NAME HERE] did not transfer alleged collection assignment rights over to [ATTORNEY FIRM NAME HERE] in order for them to collect [PLAINTIFF NAME HERE] alleged debt.

ADMISSION #12

Admit that [ATTORNEY FIRM NAME HERE] is the real party in interest.

ADMISSION #13

Admit that you cannot provide documents proving [PLAINTIFFS NAME HERE] owns this debt.

DOCUMENTS TO BE PRODUCED

STICK IT TO SUE HAPPY DEBT COLLECTORS

1. Provide the actual original credit card contract upon which your Complaint is based on, including all subsequent amended terms.

2. Provide a contract, agreement, assignment, or other means of demonstrating that the Plaintiff has the authority and was legally entitled to collect on the alleged debt.

3. Provide a copy of the Collections Assignment between [ATTORNEY FIRM HERE] and [PLAINTIFF NAME HERE].

4. Provide evidence or proof of the Defendant's alleged debt to Plaintiff, including specifically the alleged contract or agreement, between the plaintiff and defendant or any other instrument constructed solely for the purpose of creating a loan agreement between the Plaintiff and Defendant bearing Defendants signature and/or Please Produce the contract that legally requires the Defendant to pay the amount entered into complaint.

5. Provide the original or copy of the account agreement that states interest rate, grace period, finance charge, assignment, and specifically the State Laws that the agreement and account are governed plus other important facts.

6. Provide copies of the amount paid and/or the consideration due for the alleged contract/ account.

7. Provide an Itemized account of all transactions mentioned in Interrogatory Number Eighteen (18).

8. Provide the Record of Assignment that displays the information in Interrogatory No. 22.

9. Provide evidence of authorization of Plaintiff to do business, create loans, issue or extend credit, collect debts and/or operate in the State where the Plaintiff conducts their business.

10. Provide evidence of authorization of Plaintiff and Attorney to do business, create loans, issue or extend credit, collect debts and/or operate as a financial business in the State of [YOUR STATE].

11. Attach any and all notices sent to Defendant by Plaintiff in regards to this account demanding payment.

12. Attach copies of all statements generated while this alleged account was open with Plaintiff.

STICK IT TO SUE HAPPY DEBT COLLECTORS

13. Attach a complete and accurate history of the interest charged on this alleged account with Plaintiff. Show the exact dates those interest rates changed and list the various rates that were charged during the this debt and the exact method of amortization.

14. Attach any and all notices sent to Defendant by Plaintiff announcing changes in interest, fees or penalties and/or the terms of this alleged debt.

15. Identify each Credit Reporting Agency (credit bureau) to which the Plaintiff reported defendant's debt and the dates of each such report.

16. Provide the original dunning letter that was sent to Defendant.

17. Attach any and all notices sent to Defendant by Plaintiff in regards to account announcing transfer and/or assignment of credit card account from plaintiff to any collection agency or collection attorney.

18. Attach a copy of the agreement with Plaintiff that grants [ATTORNEY NAME HERE] Attorney(s) the authority to collect this alleged debt.

CERTIFICATE OF SERVICE

I hereby certify that a copy of the foregoing Request for Discovery was mailed on the [DATE: Day, Month, Year] to [ATTORNEY NAME AND ADDRESS].

_____

Defendant Pro Se

[YOUR ADDRESS, CITY, STATE, ZIP]

[YOUR PHONE NUMBER]

[NOTARY PUBLIC]

RESPONSES TO PLAINTIFFS DISCOVERY

ADMISSIONS

REMEMBER: THE GOAL IS TO MAKE THEM PROVE EVERYTHING. DO NOT HELP THEM PROVE THE CASE BY GIVING THEM ANYTHING THEY CAN USE IN DISCOVERY.

It's actually quite easy to answer Admissions and Interrogatories, Production of Documents etc., in such a way that you don't have to produce much of anything for them. Make them work to prove the case.

When you file your discovery requests you can bet that the Plaintiff's attorney is going to file discovery for you to answer, admit and produce. Be very careful how you answer the Interrogatories, Admissions, and Production of Documents. Never state "lack of information", it will give the opposing attorney the opportunity to file a motion with the court to deeming your discovery admissions admitted. Don't worry I will show you how to avoid that trap.

While I cannot cover every possible question or admission that the Plaintiffs attorney may send you, I will cover the basics and also a couple of "trick" questions that the attorney may try to use on you. When in doubt answer the admissions with "Defendant states that after a reasonable inquiry, the information known or readily obtainable by him is insufficient to enable him to admit or deny this request."

Be wary about answering admissions with "DENY" unless you are certain. For instance, the debt is not yours. If you answer with DENY or DENIED and they come back with the actual contract, credit card statements or agreement you will have problems, bet on that.

You can just answer TRUE or DENIED, however I prefer to answer them all with: *"Defendant states that after a reasonable inquiry, the information known or readily obtainable by him is insufficient to enable him to admit or deny this request."* I do this because I do not have a contract or assignment in my possession or sufficient cause to believe one hundred (100%) that I am able to answer TRUE or DENIED. (Kind of like the graduated denial, I discussed earlier).

INTERROGATORIES

I can't cover every single possible Interrogatory that an attorney may ask, just be careful when you answer anything to do with payments, methods of payments, etc. You'll notice in many of my responses to the interrogatories that I put the burden back on the Plaintiff with "Plaintiff's request should be accessible to Plaintiff from Plaintiff's own files, from documents or information already in Plaintiff's possession".

If they ask for your social security number, place of birth, bank account information etc., I would answer it as an "objection" with the statement "*[INTERROGATORY #] is objected by the Defendant on the grounds that it is personal, confidential and private. This Interrogatory seeks information that is not relevant to any issue in this action, information not calculated to lead to the discovery of admissible evidence, information not relevant to any subject matter of this action, and would result in the disclosure of information where such disclosure would violate the privacy rights of the Defendant.*"

They may also ask if you made any payments to the Plaintiff (this will not work if you made payments to a collection agency). I would answer this as an objection with the statement

"[INTERROGATORY #] is objected by the Defendant on the grounds that it is overly broad and unduly burdensome to the extent it seeks documents or records that are not within the current knowledge, possession, custody or control of the Defendant. Plaintiff's request should be accessible to Plaintiff from Plaintiff's own files, from documents or information already in Plaintiff's possession."

If they ask you to identify any payments to the original creditor or the date of the payment amount or date I would answer it as an objection with the statement *"[INTERROGATORY #] is objected by the Defendant on the grounds that it is overly broad, unduly burdensome, cumulative and/or duplicative to the extent it seeks documents or records that are not within the current knowledge, possession, custody or control of the Defendant. Plaintiff's request should be accessible to Plaintiff from Plaintiff's own files, from documents or information already in Plaintiff's possession. The Plaintiff did not attach a copy of the Alleged Contract to the Complaint, thus the probity of the requested information is speculative. The Defendant has sought the Contract Alleged through Discovery and demands strict proof thereof".*

STICK IT TO SUE HAPPY DEBT COLLECTORS

Be very wary of any interrogatories that ask you identify a payment on account XXXX-XXXX (format may be a bit different) but earlier (or later) ask you to identify a payment to an original creditor. This is a trick question, be sure to answer it as an objection with a statement *"[INTERROGATORY #] is objected by the Defendant on the grounds that it is overly broad, unduly burdensome, cumulative and/or duplicative to the extent it seeks documents or records that are not within the current knowledge, possession, custody or control of the Defendant. The Defendant has sought the Proof of Alleged Account Number and Account Stated through Discovery and demands strict proof thereof"*.

Any time money, or account information such as account number, lists of payment dates, etc. is requested be sure to object and answer as above, they will try to trick you into admitting payments, etc. by using a series of related questions. So be on your toes. The whole goal is to answer as little as possible so that the Plaintiff has the burden of proving you owe the debt.

They may ask you if the amount they are suing for is the correct amount. This is another trick question. Answer as an objection with this statement *"[INTERROGATORY #] is objected by the Defendant on the ground that it is unduly burdensome to the ex-*

tent it seeks information that is not within the current knowledge, possession, custody or control of the Defendant. Additionally, the request is premature as it requests the Defendant, prior to the completion of discovery to answer if the amount is correct. The Plaintiff should have records or documents of the Amount Sued upon as being correct from Plaintiff's own files and the Defendant has asked the Plaintiff to provide this proof such as an account stated during his discovery. And the Defendant has listed this as an Affirmative Defense in his Answer. The Defendant leaves the Plaintiff to its proof. Without waiving the Defendant's objection the defendant does not know if the amount on the alleged account he is being sued upon is correct because the Defendant has not been provided with any evidence by the Plaintiff to prove such amount is correct".

They may also ask if you made any settlement offers on the account. This is yet another trick question and should be answered with an objection with this statement "*[INTERROGATORY #] is objected by the Defendant on the grounds that it is unduly burdensome to the extent it seeks information that is not within the current knowledge, possession, custody or control of the Defendant. The Plaintiff claims to be the Owner of the alleged* account therefore the Plaintiff should have records or documents of any settlements made to Defendant from Plaintiff's own files. Without waiving the Defendant's objection, the defendant to the best of his knowledge has never received any settlement offers".

They will probably also ask if you are going to produce any witnesses or exhibits at trial in the interrogatories.

In the case of witnesses, I would answer as an objection with a statement of "*[INTERROGATORY #] is objected to the extent that it is seeking information that is premature, given that the parties are in the midst of discovery and pertinent documents have not yet been produced by the Plaintiff. The Defendant cannot possibly answer this Interrogatory when he has not seen the Plaintiff answers to his Discovery. Without waiving his objection, the Defendant at this time has no witnesses, but reserves the right to call witnesses, if need be, once the Plaintiff answers their Discovery given by the Defendant*".

In the case of exhibits, I would as an objection with a statement of "*[INTERROGATORY #] is objected as it is requesting information that it is premature given that the parties are in the midst of discovery and pertinent documents have not yet been produced by the Plaintiff".*

Lastly, they may ask you for each factual basis of the defense you now assert (your affirmative defenses). I would once again object with a statement of *"[INTERROGATORY #] is objected by the Defendant on the grounds that it is seeking information that is premature given that the parties are in the midst of discovery and pertinent documents have not yet been produced by the Plaintiff. Without waiving his objection, the Defendant upon completion of discovery with the Plaintiff, will most definitely have defenses in this action, and will provide such defenses to the Plaintiff if asked through Discovery. The Defendant reserves the right to update this answer to this interrogatory at a later time when that decision is made".*

The above interrogatory responses are the most common that I have run across, however they may ask others. Be very careful when responding to any interrogatory that involves a monetary amount, asking you to identify anything to do with an account (account number, payment dates, etc.).

WHEN IN DOUBT BE VAGUE. Use something along the lines of *"is objected by the Defendant on the grounds that it is overly broad, unduly burdensome, cumulative, and/or duplicative to the extent it seeks documents or records that are not within the current knowledge, possession, custody or control of the Defendant."*

DOCUMENT REQUESTS

The opposing attorney will try to trick you again into providing proof of the debt. While I can't outline every possible request they will make, I can cover the most common requests.

They may request something along the lines of the following:

Please provide copies of any and all payments made on the account sued upon, for example, all canceled checks, money order receipts, etc., including a copy of any payment which you allege paid off or settle the account sued upon.

I would answer the above with something to the nature of:

Defendant objects as the Plaintiff's request for [DOCUMENTS NO. #] as it assumes there is an account being sued upon where no account has been identified as of yet by the Plaintiff or its at-

torneys. It is burdensome to the extent it seeks documents or records that are that are not within the current knowledge, possession, custody or control of the Defendant, more readily or accessible to Plaintiff from Plaintiff's own files, from documents or information already in Plaintiff's possession. The Defendant cannot provide what is requested.

They may also request something along the lines of "Please provide copies of any and all settlement letters or offers to settle regarding the account sued upon".

I would answer the above with something similar to the following:

The Defendant objects as the Plaintiff's request for [DOCUMENTS NO. #] is overbroad and unduly burdensome to the extent it seeks documents or records that are that are not within the current knowledge, possession, custody or control of the Defendant, the Plaintiff claims they are the Assignee of the alleged account therefore these documents should be more readily or accessible to Plaintiff from Plaintiff's own files, from documents or information already in Plaintiff's possession. The Defendant has no documents to provide this request.

STICK IT TO SUE HAPPY DEBT COLLECTORS

They will most likely make a request such as this:

"Please provide copies of any and all receipts, letters, or other information that supports your argument the account was paid in full".

I would answer the above with:

The Defendant objects to Plaintiff's Request for [DOCUMENTS NO. #] because the Defendant never alleged that the account was paid in full, therefore cannot provide this request.

They may also request any exhibits that you may produce at trial. I would answer this request along the line of: The Defendant cannot provide Request for [Documents NO. #] because he does not have any exhibits.

They may also request something along the lines of:

Please provide copies of all notice letters, collection letters, statements and charge slips in your possession on the contract sued upon.

Again, I would answer the above with something like:

ORIGINAL CREDITOR LAWSUITS

Defendant objects to Plaintiff's request for [DOCUMENTS NO. #] on the grounds that it is burdensome, seeing it is requesting documents in regards to the contract sued upon, where no contract as of yet has been identified by the Plaintiff or their attorneys. The Defendant has nothing in his possession to provide.

As I mentioned earlier, the above are the most common request for production of documents. If they make other requests, I would suggest that you be vague about it using similar language as above.

As you may have noticed in the admissions, interrogatories and requests for documents they ask for the same information. This is a trick to help them prove their case through *your own* admissions. You need to make sure that you do not have any conflicts in any of your responses to their requests for discovery.

Debt Buyer (junk debt collectors) Lawsuits

Often time's original creditor will sell a debt to a third party for literally pennies on the dollar. I call them Junk Debt Buyers. Junk debt buyers are often more aggressive in the collection of a debt, for instance, they will be more likely to file a lawsuit. The problem is that the junk debt buyer purchased the debt for less than the amount owed and will sue for the face value of the debt. This practice is known as "unjust enrichment" and we are going to challenge this in our Answer and in subsequent legal filings.

Junk debt buyers generally do not have any documentation, such as the original agreement or amended terms, when they file suit, as the original creditor did not transfer any documents with the sale of the account. This is good for consumers as we are going

DEBT BUYER (JUNK DEBT COLLECTORS) LAWSUITS

to force their hand and make them produce documentation. The chances are very good, that after file the Motion to Dismiss they will file a voluntary dismissal and go away. If not, then I will show you how to turn up the heat to high and beat them during discovery.

There isn't much difference between an Original Creditor and a Junk Debt lawsuit. I am going to use the same outline as we did in Chapter 3 - Original Creditor Lawsuits, and add additional Affirmative Defenses and some changes in the Motion to Dismiss and discovery.

As I did with an original creditor lawsuit, I am going to deny everything in the complaint with the exception of the allegation(s) that identify me as a personally and where I live. See Chapter Three regarding "Deny Everything". Additionally with junk debt buyer lawsuits I would add additional Affirmative Defenses that pertain to debt buyers. Explanations of each Affirmative Defense are at the end of the example.

When answering a complaint you have only three options: True (admitted as true), Denied (denied as untrue), or "neither admitted true or denied because I do not enough information to know the truth of the matter".

WHEN IN DOUBT DENY IT. FORCE THE OPPOSING ATTORNEY PROVE OTHERWIS.

Answering the complaint and affirmative defenses – deny everything

ANSWER TO COMPLAINT ON ACCOUNT

My name is XXXXX XXXXXXXXXXX, and I am representing myself in this action. In response to each of the numbered paragraphs of the Plaintiff's Complaint or Petition, I state as follows:

1. The allegations of Paragraph One are: True (this is the line that had my name and place of residence on it)

2. The allegations of Paragraph Two are: Denied

3. The allegations of Paragraph Three are: Denied

4. The allegations of Paragraph Four are: Denied

DEBT BUYER (JUNK DEBT COLLECTORS) LAWSUITS

AFFIRMATIVE DEFENSES

1. Plaintiff Lacks Standing.

2. Defendant was not notified of any assignment of the debt that is the subject of the Complaint.

3. The Complaint fails to state a claim upon which relief may be granted.

4. Defendant does not consent to or ratify any assignment of the debt that is the subject of the Complaint, or any portion of it.

5. Plaintiff's Complaint is time-barred Pursuant to [YOUR STATES STATUTE OF LIMITATIONS CODE HERE]. (See explanation at the end of the example)

6. Defendant claims Lack of Privity as Defendant has never entered into any contractual or debtor/creditor arrangements with Plaintiff.

7. Plaintiff's claims are barred by the doctrine of laches.

(#8 pertains to the state of Georgia only and varies from state to state.)

8. Plaintiff's claims are barred by the statute of frauds, O.C.G.A. § 13-5-30 as the purported contract or agreement falls within a class of contracts or agreements that are required to be in writing. The purported contract alleged in the Complaint was not in writing and not signed by Defendant or by some another person authorized by Defendant and who was to answer to the alleged debt, default, or miscarriage of the other person.

9. Plaintiff's Complaint fails to allege a valid assignment of debt and there are no averments as to the nature of the purported assignment or evidence of valuable consideration.

10. Plaintiff has failed to name the Real Party in Interest.

11. Plaintiff's Complaint fails to allege that the Assignor/Original Creditor even has knowledge of this action or that the Assignor conveyed all rights and control to the Plaintiff. The record does not disclose this information and it cannot be assumed without creating an unfair prejudice against the Defendant.

12. Defendant claims Accord and Satisfaction as Defendant alleges that the original creditor accepted payment from a third party for the purported debt, or a portion of the purported debt,

or that the Original Creditor received other compensation in the form of monies or credits from the Plaintiff.

13. Plaintiff's claims are barred by the principle of waiver

14. Plaintiff's claims are based on a contract that is an adhesion contract, and as such, all or portions of it are unenforceable.

15. Plaintiff's claims are based on a contract that is illusory and therefore unenforceable.

16. Plaintiff's calculation of interest is usurious or based on a rate that is greater than allowed by law.

17. Plaintiff has failed to state a valid claim for attorney fees, and is barred from collecting Attorney fees under the Fair Debt Collection Practices Act.

18. Plaintiff is barred under the Fair Debt Collection Practices Act, from collecting attorney fees, interest, collection fees, and any amount not specifically provided for by purported agreement.

19. Plaintiff's damages are limited to real or actual damages only.

20. Plaintiff's counsel did not afford Defendant due process of the law.

21. If allowed by this court the defendant reserves the right to plead other affirmative defenses that may become available at a later time.

Date

Signed

[NOTARY PUBLIC]

Explanations of the Affirmative Defenses

1. Plaintiff Lacks Standing - The ability of a party to demonstrate to the court sufficient connection to and harm from the law or action challenged to support that party's participation in the case. In the United States, the current doctrine is that a person cannot bring a suit challenging the constitutionality of a law unless the Plaintiff can demonstrate that the plaintiff is (or will imminently be) harmed by the law. Otherwise, the court will rule that the plaintiff "lacks standing" to bring the suit, and will dismiss the case without considering the merits of the claim of unconstitutionality. In order to sue to have a court declare a law unconstitutional, there must be a valid

DEBT BUYER (JUNK DEBT COLLECTORS) LAWSUITS

reason for whoever is suing to be there. The party suing must have something to lose in order to sue unless they have automatic standing by action of law.

2. You were not given a copy of the assignment that they are claiming they own. You were not aware that the Plaintiff bought the debt from the original creditor and this is the first you've heard of it.
3. Claim for Relief – The Plaintiff did not attach proper evidence or claim to the complaint. They cannot prove any set of facts in support of their claim that would entitle them to relief.
4. That you do not consent or approve of any portion of the alleged assignment that supposedly exists in the complaint.
5. Every state has a statute of limitations on how long a person can wait to sue over a debt. You will need to check your state laws regarding statute of limitations. You can either search via a search engine or look it up at the local library in their law section.
6. The doctrine of privity in contract law provides that a contract cannot confer rights or impose obligations arising under it on any person or agent except the parties to it. Only parties to contracts should be able to sue to enforce their rights or claim damages as such. The doctrine of privity has been proven to be problematic due to its implications upon contracts made for the benefit of third parties who are unable to enforce the obligations of the contracting parties
7. Barred by the Doctrine of Laches - Doctrine of Laches limits the legal claim of a person, by virtue of any undue delay on

his part in enforcing his legal right. (Remember, they only attached a single boilerplate agreement and they improperly filed a Suit on Account instead of a Breach of Contract).
8. Barred by the Statute of Frauds – This is a requirement that certain contracts (such as for sale of land, sale of goods exceeding a certain value, a debt guaranty) must be in writing and properly executed to prevent fraud and perjury. Otherwise such contracts cannot be enforced in the courts although they remain legal (are not rendered void). The statute of frauds varies from state to state.
9. The plaintiff has no valid assignment of debt and that there is no evidence or facts to back up the details underlying it
10. The Plaintiff has not proven that they have the authority to sue you. They did not provide you with an Assignment of Debt from the Original Creditor showing that the Original Creditor signed over their rights to your account.
11. That the Assignment (if it wasn't authenticated by the original creditor) does not show exactly what the Plaintiff is entitled to, or that the assignment was not evidenced and the original creditor did not assign their rights, nor do they have knowledge of the lawsuit. Briefly, you have not been given proper proof that the debt was actually assigned to the Plaintiff, and if it was assigned it isn't showing you what the Plaintiff's rights are per that assignment.
12. A third person may give something in satisfaction of a party's debt. An accord and satisfaction is in effect if the creditor accepts the offer and the debtor authorizes, participates in, or later agrees to, the transaction. (i.e. the original

creditor sells the debt to another party). An accord and satisfaction is a contract, and all the essential elements of a contract must be present. The agreement must include a definite offer of settlement and an unconditional acceptance of the offer according to its terms. It must be final and definite, closing the matter it covers, and must leave nothing unsettled or open to question.

13. The agreement may call for full payment or some compromise and it's not necessarily based on an earlier agreement of the parties. It does not necessarily have to be in writing unless it comes within the Statute of Frauds. Unless there are matters intentionally left outside the accord and satisfaction, it settles the entire controversy between the parties. It extinguishes all the obligations arising out of the underlying contract or tort. Where only one of two or more parties on one side settles, this ordinarily operates to discharge all of them. The reason for this rule is that there should be only one satisfaction for a single injury or wrong. This rule does not apply where the satisfaction is neither given nor accepted with the intention that it settles the entire matter.

14. Principle of Waiver - According to Black's Law Dictionary, the equitable principle of waiver is defined as "the intentional or voluntary relinquishment of a known right," a "renunciation, repudiation, abandonment, or surrender of some claim, right, privilege, or of the opportunity to take advantage of some defect, irregularity, or wrong."

15. Contract that is an Adhesion Contract - A contract of adhesion is a standard form contract, prepared by one party and

presented to the weaker party, usually a consumer who has no bargaining power and little or no choice about its terms." ~ BLACKS LAW DICTIONARY (7th Ed.) p.318. - Credit Card contracts of adhesion have been found unconscionable and unenforceable. Discover Bank v. Superior Court of Los Angeles Cal 4th 2005 Cal. LEXIS 6686.

16. Contract that is illusory and therefore unenforceable. (Remember, they only attached the boilerplate agreement and not subsequent amended terms of the agreement, chances are they'll never be able to provide 100% of the agreement, thus it doesn't in reality exist).
17. Calculation of interest is usurious – basically they jacked up the interest rate (universal default) and that the interest rate is way above legal limits. (With the enacted CARD Act of 2009, this is very important, as they may have broken the law).
18. Plaintiff has failed to state a valid claim for attorney fees, and is barred from collecting Attorney fees under the Fair Debt Collection Practices Act. – Pretty much self-explanatory.
19. Plaintiff is barred under the Fair Debt Collection Practices Act – This may or may not float as the plaintiff is supposedly the original creditor (unless it was never transferred back to them form the Asset Backed Securities).
20. They should only be compensated the amount in which they paid the Original Creditor. Actual damages are real damages to compensate for loss or injuries that have actually occurred. When damages, which have been suffered by

someone as a result of another's wrongdoing, can be precisely measured, they are called actual damages. When an original creditor sells a debt to a third party it is generally sold for less than the face value of the debt, often times just pennies on the dollar. However the junk debt buyer will often file a lawsuit for the face value of the debt, rather than what they actually paid for it. This is known as "Unjust Enrichment".
21. Plaintiff's counsel did not afford Defendant due process of the law – In my case I sent request for debt validation via certified mail, under the FDCPA they should have stopped collection efforts until such time that they provided the validation (proof) of the debt.
22. This one leaves the door open for me to file more defenses should the need arise.

Other Affirmative Defenses

The following are additional Affirmative Defenses that may apply to you.

The Plaintiff has not proven that they are authorized and licensed to collect claims for others in the State of [YOUR STATE], solicit the right to collect or receive payment of a claim of another.

You will need to check with your state laws to see if debt collectors have to be licensed and/or bonded to do business as a debt collector. Many states do not require debt collectors to be licensed and/or bonded. This affirmative defense only applies to states that do.

The Complaint fails to allege or prove that the Plaintiff is licensed and has procured a bond in the State of YOUR STATE as required.

Again this only applies to states that require debt collectors to be licensed and/or bonded. This affirmative defense only applies to states that do.

The Motion to Dismiss and Sworn Denial Bombshell

Filing a Motion to Dismiss in a junk debt collector lawsuit is very similar to the original creditor lawsuit Motion to Dismiss. In my response to junk debt buyer lawsuits, I don't use the asset backed securities Improper Plaintiff tactic. However, I do use the Federal Truth in Lending Act tactic.

Before going any further be sure to read: Filing a Motion to Dismiss and Sworn Denials in Chapter 3. It covers information that I use in both original creditor and junk debt buyer motions to dismiss.

DEBT BUYER (JUNK DEBT COLLECTORS) LAWSUITS

After reading Chapter 3 you may notice that the junk debt buyer Motion to Dismiss below does not contain the asset backed securities or the Federal Truth in Lending motion sections. If the junk debt buyer has included the name of the original creditor, you could add them to your junk debt buyer Motion to Dismiss. I haven't tested these in a junk debt buyer Motion to Dismiss, however such inclusions may help trigger a voluntary dismissal by the opposing attorney because, and in order to respond they would have to "prove" that there is no factual basis to that motion. Being that they are junk debt buyers, you can bet the original creditor did not transfer that information with the debt purchase. If you use the asset backed securities in the motion make sure you research the Prospectus to make sure that there is no language stating that the defaulted (or delinquent) account is transferred back the originator (the issuing bank).

The Truth in Lending Portion might work, especially if the junk debt buyer didn't attach the original agreement or the amended agreement terms to the complaint and summons.

At the same time that I file the Motion to Dismiss, I also file a graduated Sworn Denial. *See the example on the following page.*

SWORN DENIAL

I deny that this is my debt and if it is my debt, I deny that it is still valid debt and if it is a valid debt, I deny the amount sued for in the amount of $X,XXX.XX principal, $X,XXX.XX as interest including attorney fees is the correct amount.

[DATE]

[YOUR NAME]

_____

Signed

[NOTARY PUBLIC]

MOTION TO DISMISS

As you will see below most of what I wrote about earlier is included. Some of the items may or may not pertain to you (unless you live in the State of Georgia). You will need to search and replace to fit your needs. Some items below may not pertain to your motion, if they don't then do not used them. Motions to Dismiss should be simple, clear and to the point.

DEBT BUYER (JUNK DEBT COLLECTORS) LAWSUITS

MOTION TO DISMISS

MEMORANDUM OF POINTS AND AUTHORITIES

Comes now the Defendant [FULL NAME], and files this Request for Dismissal of Complaint, as follows:

1. The Causes of Action specified in the complaint filed by the Plaintiff is insufficient as a matter of law.

The complaint does not set forth the True facts upon which Plaintiff seeks a summary judgment. The complaint should be dismissed.

2. Defendant received the Plaintiff's Complaint on or about XXXXXXXXX XX, 200X. Defendant answered the complaint on or about XXXXXXXXXXX X, 200X.

3. Defendant on or about XXXX XX, 200X requested in writing to Plaintiff's counsel to show proof of debt (debt validation request). To date neither Plaintiff nor counsel has responded to Defendant's request to show proof of debt.

4. Plaintiff has not proved or established that I am the person who applied for or used this credit card. Defendant has issued a

Sworn Denial in this matter. First requisite element of debt is the existence of obligation. Ernst v. Jessie L. Riddle PC, MD La 1997.

Davis v. Discover Bank, 277 Ga. App. 864
Davis did not deny use of card but that Davis did not sign a contract.

5. Plaintiff has attached a credit card agreement to the complaint that has a machine typed copyright date of 2005 and a handwritten 4-1-2005 to 6-30-2008 notation. The customer agreement attached to this Suit on Account is not the agreement in effect when this account was opened nor have any amended card agreements that pertain to this class of account have been attached. (*Sometimes a junk debt attorney will attach a card statement or portions of an agreement, but not the original agreement or amended terms, you may need to re-word this section*).

7. A variety of interest rates and fees may have been applied to this account over its lifetime. The attached agreement does not specify the interest rate charged or the fee charges. These documents were issued separately from the agreement as is the

custom of card issuers. These documents have not been attached.

8. Plaintiff cannot recover interest or fees absent proof of an agreement to pay interest or fees.

(#9 *May not apply unless they file a "Suit on Account" complaint*)

9. Plaintiff is suing as Suit On Account. The elements of the account stated cause of action expressly draw a distinction between suits that grow out of course of dealing and suits that grow out of an express agreement. Cental Ntl Bank of San Angelo v. Cox 96, S.W. 2nd. 746,748. The court said:

- The cases are legion on what constitutes an account stated. In general the essential elements are: Transactions between the parties which give rise to an indebtedness of one to the other; an agreement expressed or implied, between them fixing the amount due: and a promise, express or implied, by the one to be charged, to pay such indebtedness.
- The first and defining element of the claim is the existence of a debtor-creditor relationship that arises from a series of transactions – from a course of dealing, not a

contract. This element is identical across all suits on account, whether open, sworn or stated.

An account stated theory may have been appropriate when credit card issuers gave card holders fixed interest rates and charged very few fees. With the proliferation of credit cards over the last two decades, however interest rates have varied and fees have increased in number and severity.

This suit only lists indebtedness in the amount $X,XXX.XX principal, and interest of $X,XXX.XX which works out to a simple interest rate of XX.X%. There is no notation of fees. A detailed account of the charges, interest and fees are required as Plaintiff cannot recover interest or fees absent proof of an agreement to pay interest or fees. Statements are evidence of interest rate that was actually charged NOT the rate that the parties agreed to. Tully v. Citibank (South Dakota) N.A. 173 S.W 3d 212,216 2005 and Hay v. Citibank (South Dakota) N.A., 2006 WL 2620089. Absent proof of agreed upon rate, Plaintiff should not be awarded damages based upon failure to pay the rates demanded in the monthly statements.

DEBT BUYER (JUNK DEBT COLLECTORS) LAWSUITS

The Federal Truth in Lending Act requires material terms of a credit card relationship to set forth in a written agreement. Federal Law mandates comprehensive disclosures of these terms when the account is opened and when the account is amended. The precise content and format of the disclosures that must be made in connection with every credit card application is dictated in great detail by 1607 of the Act and the implementing regulation found at 12 C.F.R. 225.5 The basic terms for which disclosure is required include:

- The annual percentage (%) rate applicable to the purchase, cash advances and balance transfers made using the account.
- The manner in which variable rates are determined.
- The amounts of annual fees or other fees for the issuance or availability of the card.
- The amounts of minimum finance charges and transaction charges.
- The existence and duration of a grace period, if any.
- The name of the balance calculation method and the amount of cash advance fees, late payment fees, over the limit fees and balance transfer fees 12 C.F.R. 225.5a(b)

The Act defined the manner and timing of such disclosures regardless of the manner in which the credit card offer is made, whether it is made by mail, telephone, in a catalog, magazine or other publication or over the internet. 15 U.S.C. § 1637(c) (1)-(7).

Additional disclosures are required in monthly statements, 12 C.F.R. 266.7, when the terms of the agreement are changed, 12 C.F.R. 226.9 (c) and before the card renewal date, 12 C.F R. 226.9 (e).

Because these disclosures are required to be in writing and integrated into the account opening process regardless of how the account is opened, the disclosed terms become defacto terms of the card agreement.

Title 15 U.S.C. § 1642 (Issuance of Credit Cards) prohibits the gratuitous issuance of a credit card. Credit card is to be issued only in response to an application or request. Any such application or request is governed by the disclosure provisions of Title 15 § U.S.C. 1637 (Open end consumer credit plans).

DEBT BUYER (JUNK DEBT COLLECTORS) LAWSUITS

It is impossible to lawfully establish a credit card account without a comprehensive written document setting forth virtually all of the material terms of the agreement.

Allowing Plaintiff to sue on account stated theory to imply an agreement to pay interest and fees stated relieves him from establishing the amount of interest and fees that were disclosed under Federal Law and that were included in the terms of its express agreement, permitting Plaintiff an unjustified windfall or unjust enrichment.

10. Breach of Contract

Georgia Law has upheld that a credit card account is a simple contract. Hill v. American Express 289 Ga. 576 657 S.E. 2nd. 547.

Plaintiff is limited to only what can be pleaded and proved under the written contract. Truly v. Austin, 744 S.w. 2nd. 934,936 (Tex 1988)

A schedule of the charges, interest and fees are required as Plaintiff cannot recover interest or fees absent proof of an agreement to pay interest or fees.

11. This is a contract of adhesion, "A contract of adhesion is a standard form contract, prepared by one party and presented to the weaker party, usually a consumer who has no bargaining power and little or no choice about its terms." BLACKS LAW DICTIONARY (7th Ed.) p. 318.

Historically Georgia courts have held that in contracts of adhesion the party who has little to no control of the terms of the contract is to be favored.

12. Credit Card contracts of adhesion have been found unconscionable and unenforceable. Discover Bank v. Superior Court of Los Angeles Cal 4th 2005 Cal. LEXIS 6686.

Congress acknowledged the abuse of contract that allowed for Universal Default, interest rate changes at will and at will fee charges with the enacted Credit Card Reform Act (CARD Act) of 2009.

13. A contract cannot be enforced if its terms are incomplete, vagur, indefiniter or uncertain. In addition the party asserting the existence of a contract has the burden of proving its existence and its term. This proof must be clear and convincing.

DEBT BUYER (JUNK DEBT COLLECTORS) LAWSUITS

Cumberland Center Assoc. v. Southeast Mgnt Ect Corp 228 Ga. App. 571-575 (1) 492 Se2d 546 (1997)

14. Plaintiffs' counsel committed fraud upon the court by filing the Suit on Account.

WHEREFORE, Defendant, [FULL NAME], respectfully submits that the Court should dismiss and deny the Plaintiff's complaint, filed herein [PLAINTIFF NAME HERE]. and prays for Dismissal of the complaint by the Plaintiff.

Defendant's Request submitted this XX day, of XXXXXXXX 200X.

_____

Defendant pro se

Address: Street address, City State, Zip

Telephone: (XXX) XXX-XXXX

[NOTARY PUBLIC]

(Along with this I included a verification and certificate of service)

Along with the Motion to Dismiss I also included a judge's order for dismissal (to make it easier for the judge, many times this is required in a Motion to Dismiss filing).

ORDER FOR DISMISSAL

WHEREFORE, in consideration of Defendant's Motion for Dismissal, it is hereby ORDERED and ADJUCATED that Defendant's motion shall be granted.

SO ORDERED this _____ day of _____, 200X.

_____

JUDGE [STATE OR COUNTY COURT and YOUR COUNTY]

DEBT BUYER (JUNK DEBT COLLECTORS) LAWSUITS

Example Verification

VERIFICATION

Personally appeared before me the undersigned who on oath states that the facts set forth in this MOTION TO DISMISS are true and correct to the best of her knowledge and belief.

_____,

Defendant pro se

[NOTARY PUBLIC]

Example Certificate of Service

CERTIFICATE OF SERVICE

I hereby certify that I have this day served the foregoing MOTION TO DISMISS upon counsel for all parties, by depositing a copy of same in the United States mail in an envelope with sufficient postage thereon addressed as follows:

STICK IT TO SUE HAPPY DEBT COLLECTORS

[ATTORNEY'S NAME and MAILING ADDRESS]

This XX day of XXXXX 200X.

_____
Defendant

Address: [Street address, city, state, zip]
Phone: (XXX) XXX-XXXXX

[NOTARY PUBLIC]

Remember that you must send a copy of the certificate of service and the Motion to Dismiss to the opposing attorney via certified mail. Be sure to have all copies of the motion, verification and certificate of service time-stamped at the court clerk's office. Anything you file with the court clerk should be notarized, even original copies that you send to the opposing attorney.

In most cases after the opposing attorney reads through the Motion to Dismiss, he or she will see that you aren't playing games and that you are fighting them tooth and nail. If the opposing attorney knows they can't respond with proper documentation as you outlined in the Motion to Dismiss, he will most likely abandon the lawsuit by filing a voluntary dismissal. Debt collection attorneys want easy money they get from default judgments. They will rarely work hard if they know they have an uphill battle ahead of them to prove their case. This is to your advantage when being sued.

In rare cases the Plaintiff attorney will attempt to respond to your Motion to Dismiss (most won't). If they do and the judge denies your motion, we file a couple of things and force the Plaintiff's attorney to produce documentation such as the original agreement and any amended agreement terms (remember the Truth In Lending Act), answer questions (Interrogatories) and to admit or deny facts in the case (Request for Admissions).

You may need to do research (your state laws) and make changes to the Motion to Dismiss so that it properly and accurately fit your needs.

Motion to Strike Affidavit of Debt or Affidavit of Account

Often times the opposing attorney will file what is called an Affidavit of Debt or Affidavit of Account that is attested to and alleged by an employee of the original creditor. It is important that a motion to strike is filed as in many cases the "employee" is an employee of the law firm not an employee of original creditor. The affidavit is one hundred percent (100%) hearsay. In order to prevent them from using an affidavit of debt we need to file what is called a motion to strike.

When an attorney files an Affidavit of Debt or Account it will have a corresponding Exhibit (such as Exhibit A, Exhibit B, etc.). We will need that in order to file a motion to strike the affidavit. Most judges look at these sorts of affidavits as hearsay anyway, but we need to file a motion to strike in any case.

Example of a Motion to Strike Affidavit of Debt

DEFENDANT'S MOTION TO STRIKE PLAINTIFF'S AFFIDAVIT OF DEBT

Now comes the Defendant [YOUR FULL NAME HERE], who requests this Honorable Court to Strike the Plaintiff's Affidavit of Debt for the Following Reasons:

1. The Plaintiff has file [EXHIBIT] Affidavit of debt.

DEBT BUYER (JUNK DEBT COLLECTORS) LAWSUITS

2. [EXHIBIT] affidavit pertains to acts and events that allegedly occurred between Defendant and a third party, [ORIGINAL CREDITORS NAME].

3. At no time was the creator of the affidavit nor any of the original creditors employees present to witness Any alleged acts or creation of the records of transactions occurring between defendant and the [ORIGINAL CREDITORS NAME or PLAINTIFFS NAME].

4. As such said affidavit falls under the hearsay rule [YOUR STATES EVIDENCE RULE HERE] and is inadmissible as evidence. (*Georgia Law Rules of Evidence are covered under O.C.G.A. Title 24*)

5. Defendant further states that the affidavit is not subject to the hearsay business records exemption because it was not made at or near the time of the alleged acts or evens, and;

6. The information contained in the document is merely an accumulation of hearsay, and;

7. Upon Information and belief, the creator of the document in Plaintiff's [EXHIBIT] is not currently and has never been em-

ployed with [ORIGINAL CREDITORS NAME] and therefore cannot have personal knowledge of how [ORIGINAL CREDITORS NAME] records were prepared and maintained and;

8. Is unqualified to testify as to the truth of the information contained in Plaintiff's [EXHIBIT].

WHEREFORE, the Defendant prays that the Plaintiff's [EXHIBIT] be stricken from the evidence in the above action.

Defendant's Request submitted this XX day, of XXXXXXXX 200X.

Respectfully Submitted,

_____

[YOUR NAME HERE]
Defendant Pro Se

[YOUR FULL ADDRESS HERE]
[PHONE NUMBER HERE]

[NOTARY PUBLIC]

DEBT BUYER (JUNK DEBT COLLECTORS) LAWSUITS

You should also include a Judge's Order, Verification and Certificate of Service. Remember that you must send a copy of the certificate of service and the motion to strike to the opposing attorney via certified mail. Be sure to have all copies of the motion, verification and certificate of service time-stamped at the court clerk's office. Be sure to have the motion to strike, verification and certificate notarized (all copies).

ORDER FOR MOTION TO STRIKE AFFIDAVIT OF DEBT

WHEREFORE, in consideration of Defendant's Motion to Strike Affidavit of Debt, it is hereby ORDERED and ADJUCATED that Defendant's motion shall be granted.

SO ORDERED this _____ day of _____, 200X.

_____

JUDGE
[STATE OR COUNTY COURT and YOUR COUNTY]

Example Verification

VERIFICATION

Personally appeared before me the undersigned who on oath states that the facts set forth in this MOTION TO STRIKE AFFIDAVIT OF DEBT are true and correct to the best of her knowledge and belief.

_____,

Defendant pro se

[NOTARY PUBLIC]

DEBT BUYER (JUNK DEBT COLLECTORS) LAWSUITS

Example Certificate of Service

CERTIFICATE OF SERVICE

I hereby certify that I have this day served the foregoing MOTION TO DISMISS upon counsel for all parties, by depositing a copy of same in the United States mail in an envelope with sufficient postage thereon addressed as follows:

[ATTORNEY'S NAME and MAILING ADDRESS]

This XX day of XXXXX 200X.

_____

Defendant

Address: [Street address, city, state, zip]
Phone: (XXX) XXX-XXXXX

[NOTARY PUBLIC]

Discovery - Interrogatories, Request for Production of Documents, Request for Admissions

Before going any further read: Discovery in Chapter 3. It covers information that I use in both original creditor and junk debt buyer Discovery (Interrogatories, Admissions, and Requests for Documents).

Filing for Discovery is basically the same in junk debt buyer lawsuits as it is in original creditor lawsuits. There are a couple of additional Admissions, Interrogatories, and Document Requests that I add to junk debt buyer lawsuit Discovery.

Example of Discovery

(Interrogatories, Request for Documents, and Request for Admissions)

INSTRUCTIONS AND DEFINITIONS

1. For the purposes of these discovery requests, the following definitions apply:

A. "Defendant" means [YOUR FULL NAME]. The alleged original creditor is [ORIGINAL CREDITOR NAME HERE]; and the account means any alleged account related to the debt.

DEBT BUYER (JUNK DEBT COLLECTORS) LAWSUITS

B. "Plaintiff" or "Plaintiffs" refer to [PLAINTIFFS NAME HERE] as well as any person in their agency or employ.

C. "Creditor" refers to as well as any person in their agency or employ.

D. "FDCPA" refers to the Fair Debt collection Practices act in its entirety.

E. "Document" as used herein means, original, copies of original, or copies of any records, minutes, notices, books, papers, contracts, memoranda, invoices, correspondence, notes, calendars, photographs, drawings, charts, graphs other writings, recording tapes, recording discs, mechanical or electronic information storage or recording elements (including any information stored on a computer), written and recorded telephone messages, and any other "documents". If a document has been prepared in several copies, or additional copies have been made that are not identical (or are no longer identical due to subsequent notation or other modification of any kind whatsoever, including without limitation notations on the backs of pages thereof) each non-identical copy is a separate document.

F. "And", "or", and "and/or" shall be construed as broadly as possible so that information otherwise within the scope of the request is not excluded.

G. "Statement" or "Statements" means the periodic monthly statement issued by the plaintiff

H. "Assignment Agreement" includes but is not limited to bills of sale, the actual purchase and assignment agreement document(s) including the terms and conditions of the sale, and the schedule of accounts included in sale. Assignment Agreements shall also mean the complete documentation of the chain of custody between the original creditor and plaintiff.

I. "Application" means the document or documents submitted to the original creditor for the purposes of acquiring the account.

J. "Person" includes natural persons, corporations, partnerships, associations, or any type of entity, and agents, servants, employees, and representatives thereof.

K. The "debt" means the alleged debt that is the subject of this lawsuit.

DEBT BUYER (JUNK DEBT COLLECTORS) LAWSUITS

L. The term "identify", when used in reference to an individual person or business entity means to state the person's or entity's full name, and if applicable, present occupation or position, professional qualifications, employer, employees, present business address, and present and past business affiliations with or relationships to any of the parties in this action known.

M. When used in reference to a document, "identify" means to describe the type of document (e.g., "letter"), date, author and addressee, to state the location of the documents and the name, address and relationship to each party in this action of each and every person who has such document in his or her possession, custody or control.

N. "Attorney" means [ATTORNEY NAME HERE]. Or any other [YOUR STATE] Licensed Attorney employed by [ATTORNEYS FIRM NAME HERE].

O. When answering the Interrogatories, you must furnish all requested information, not subject to valid objection that is known by, possessed by, or available to you or your subsidiaries, employers, employees, managers, attorneys, consultants, agents, or representatives.

P. If you are unable to fully answer any of these Interrogatories, please answer them to the fullest extent possible, specify the reasons for your inability to further answer and state whatever information, knowledge or belief that you have concerning the portion not fully answered.

Q. Each numbered subpart of a numbered Interrogatory is to be considered a separate interrogatory for the purpose of objection. Thus, you must object separately to each subpart; and if you object to less than all of the subparts of a numbered interrogatory, answer the remaining subparts.

R. If any information called for in these Interrogatories is withheld on the ground that such information is for any reason exempt from discovery, then:

1. . State the ground or grounds for withholding such information;
2. Describe the type of information being withheld;
3. Identify all persons who have knowledge of the information being withheld;

4. Furnish such other information as may be required to enable the court to adjudicate the propriety of your refusal to furnish such information;

S. You are under a duty to reasonably supplement your response to each question directly addressed to the identity and locations of persons having knowledge of discoverable matters, and other information that may come to you in the future.

1. For persons, state the person's name, residence address, business address, telephone number, and the name of his/her employer;

2. For entities, state the name and address of its principal place of business, telephone number (if the person's entity's present address in known, please give his/her last known address);

3. For documents, state the author, addressee and recipient, date, a general description, a brief summary of its contents, the name and address of the custodian or the original, or best copy, any other descriptive information necessary in order to adequately describe it in a subpoena duces tecum or in a request or motion for its production.

In lieu of such identification, you may attach a copy of each document to your answer to these interrogatories;

4. For oral communications, state exactly what was said, when, where, by whom, to whom, and who else was in hearing distance; and identify all documents that mention, relate to, or have any connection with each such communications.

5. Whenever appropriate in these discovery requests, the singular and plural forms of words shall be interpreted interchangeably so as to bring within the scope of these requests any matter which might otherwise be construed outside their scope.

6. Unless otherwise indicated, these discovery requests apply to the time period commencing when the Defendant allegedly opened the account, through the present;

7. Except as expressly provided in a particular discovery request, all of the terms utilized in these discovery requests shall have the meaning given to them in the Georgia Rules of Civil Procedure.

DEBT BUYER (JUNK DEBT COLLECTORS) LAWSUITS

CLAIMS OF PRIVILEGE

If an objection to a request is based upon a claim of privilege or attorney work product, identify each document so withheld. With regard to all documents or portions of documents withheld on this basis, identify its creator; provide a brief description of the document, and state with particularity the basis of the claim of privilege, work product, or other ground of nondisclosure.

LOST OR DESTROYED DOCUMENTS

If any document requested has been lost, discarded, or destroyed, identify such document. State the type of document, its date, the approximate date it was lost, discarded, or destroyed, the reason it was lost, discarded or destroyed, a summary of its substance, and the identity of each person having knowledge of the contents thereof.

INTERROGATORIES

INTERROGATORY #1

Is [PLAINTIFFS NAME HERE] the direct assignee of [ORIGINAL CREDITOR NAME HERE]? Or, is [PLAINTIFFS NAME HERE] an assignee of an assignee? If there are additional assignees, identify each assignee, their business address, and telephone number.

INTERROGATORY #2

Identify when the alleged account was originally opened by the defendant and was subsequently charged off by [ORIGINAL CREDITOR].

INTERROGATORY #3

Identify the person or persons answering these interrogatories. Include their business address, business phone number, and title within the Plaintiff's Organization.

INTERROGATORY #4

Provide the following information for each person known to the Plaintiff who has knowledge of facts relevant to this case, including but not limited to all persons interviewed by you, by your counsel, or by any person cooperating with you in the this action, giving a brief description thereof, for each person you may call as a witness in this case.

 1. Name, address, and telephone number.

2. Place of Employment

3. Relation to the Plaintiff

4. The subjects and substance of the testimony the witness will give; and whether the witness is to be tendered as an expert witness.

INTERROGATORY #5

Provide the following information.

1. Your Full Name
2. Your Full Business Name
3. Your Business Purpose (e.g. Creditor, Lender, Collection Agency, etc.)
4. Form of Business Organization (e.g. corporation, partnership, LLC, sole proprietorship, etc.)

INTERROGATORY #6

In regards to the contract or agreement alleged in this action, please state the following:

1. Terms of the Contract or Agreement:

2. Credit Limit Amount Financed in the Alleged Contract or Agreement:
3. Date and Monetary value of any valuable consideration received on the contract or agreement:
4. Date and Monetary value of any payments or credits alleged to be executed on the contract or agreement:

INTERROGATORY #7

Provide the following information for each person who has had any involvement in any manner in any efforts on your behalf to collect or attempt to collect any debt (s) purportedly owing by Defendant.

1. His/Her Position

2. His/Her work address, telephone numbers

3. Nature and purpose of his/her involvement.

INTERROGATORY #8

Identify the persons or entities, regarding any debt(s), which you have attempted to collect from Defendant, identify all documents related or relevant to your contractual agreement(s) (Servicing,

Assignment(s), etc.), or other business relationships with said persons or entities.

INTERROGATORY #9

Plaintiff and Attorney. Please Identify each person who has had any contact or communication on your behalf regarding Defendant's purported debt(s), state when, how, where, and with whom said contact or communication occurred and in detail and with particularity the substance thereof.

INTERROGATORY #10

Attorney. Describe all collection activities, which you were authorized to perform for [PLAINTIFF NAME HERE], and identify the terms of the agreement between [PLAINTIFF NAME HERE] and you pursuant to which you sought to collect this account.

INTERROGATORY #11

Describe [PLAINTIFFS NAME HERE] procedure and policy with respect to the Maintenance, preservation, and destruction of documents, stating in your Answer whether any documents or things relating to any information Requested in these interrogatories, or related in any way to this lawsuit, have ever been destroyed or are no longer in your custody. For each such doc-document, please identify the document, how, when and why each document was destroyed or otherwise left your control, the identity of any person who participated in any way in the destruction and/or action for destroying the document or to transfer it out of your control or custody; and if the document still exists, identify the person now having control or custody of the document.

INTERROGATORY #12

What document states in writing in support of your Complaint that the Defendant is indebted to pay the Plaintiff and when was this agreed statement in writing entered into?

INTERROGATORY #13

On what date did the defendant become indebted to the plaintiff for $[AMOUNT HERE] plus accrued interest of $[INTEREST AMOUNT HERE]?

INTERROGATORY #14

Identify all witnesses with evidence in support of your Complaint that the Defendant, entered into a contract and is indebted to the Plaintiff.

INTERROGATORY #15

State all actions taken to verify the accuracy and completeness of the accounts reported and state your procedures designed to assure the maximum possible accuracy of the information reported by you.

INTERROGATORY #16

What is the date that the defendant allegedly defaulted on the original account?

INTERROGATORY #17

What was the status of the alleged contract/account when acquired?

INTERROGATORY #18

What credit card purchases and/or cash advances made on this account? When and where were they made?

INTERROGATORY #18

Please identify and describe each exhibit you will use in the trial of [CIVIL ACTION NUMBER HERE]

INTERROGATORY #19

State fully, completely and at length the factual basis of each defense, which you now assert or intend to assert in this action.

INTERROGATORY #20

As to each defense set out in response to Interrogatory Nineteen (19), above, state the following as to notification to Defendant of such defenses; (a) the date or dates when notification was given; (b) the manner in which notification was given; and (c) the specific party or parties to whom notification was given.

INTERROGATORY #21

How much was this account purchased for from [ORIGINAL CREDITOR]?

INTERROGATORY #22

DEBT BUYER (JUNK DEBT COLLECTORS) LAWSUITS

Do you have the Actual Contract between the Defendant and [ORIGINAL CREDITOR]? In addition to do you have the Assignment Agreement between [ORIGINAL CREDITOR NAME] and [PLAINTIFF NAME HERE]?

REQUEST FOR ADMISSIONS

The Defendant requests that the Plaintiff answer the following requests for Admissions pursuant to, and in accordance with, Georgia Rules of Civil Procedure O.C.G.A. § 9-11-36. If the Plaintiff objects to any requested admission, the reason therefore shall be stated. The Plaintiff's answer shall specifically admit or deny the requested admission, or set forth in detail the reasons why the Plaintiff cannot truthfully admit or deny the requested admission. A denial shall fairly meet the substance of the requested admission, and when good faith requires that the Plaintiff qualify an answer or deny only in part of the matter of which an admission is requested, the Plaintiff shall specify so much of it as is true and qualify or deny the remainder, again detailing the specificity of the denial of the part thereof.

Admit that you were not assigned [ORIGINAL CREDTOR NAME] obligations under the purchase agreement.

ADMISSION #1

Admit that you do not have the original or a copy of an assignment between you and [ORIGINAL CREDITOR NAME].

ADMISSION #2

Admit that there was no written agreement, signed by Defendant, between Defendant and [ORIGINAL CREDITOR NAME].

ADMISSION #3

Admit that there is no written agreement between [PLAINTIFF] and the Defendant.

ADMISSION #4

Admit that in the state of Georgia defendant is authorized to pay the Original Creditor/Lender until he receives notification of assignment of rights to payment, and that payment is to be made to the assignee.

ADMISSION #5

Admit that in the state of Georgia, that if requested by the debtor, the assignee must seasonably furnish reasonable proof that the assignment has been made and unless he does so the debtor may pay the original lender.

ADMISSION #6

Admit that you did not send the defendant any notification of assignment of the account or assignment of rights.

ADMISSION #7

Admit that as of the date you drafted your Complaint, you had no evidence admissible at trial that proves Defendant owes the debt.

ADMISSION #8

Admit that [PLAINTIFF NAME HERE] are considered Debt collectors under the Fair Debt Collection Practices Act.

ADMISSION #9

Admit that you are barred under the Fair Debt Collection Practices Act, U.S.C. 15 § 1692 f(1) from collecting interest on any amount not authorized by the agreement creating the debt or permitted by law.

ADMISSION #10

Admit that you do not have the agreement to claim the amount(s) submitted in the complaint.

ADMISSION #11

Admit that you do not have a copy of or the original [ORIGINAL CREDITOR NAME HERE] Cardholder Agreement.

ADMISSION #12

Admit that you did not transfer your alleged assignment rights over to [ATTORNEY FIRM NAME HERE] in order for them to collect your alleged debt.

ADMISSION #13

Admit that [ATTORNEYS NAME HERE] is the real party in interest.

ADMISSION #14

Admit that if you did purchase the alleged account it was in default.

ADMISSION #15

Admit that if this assignment is proven by you it was purchased for less than the amount submitted in your complaint.

ADMISSION #16

Admit that no notification of attempt to collect on this debt was sent to the following address by [ORIGINAL CREDITOR NAME HERE]: [YOUR FULL ADDRESS HERE].

ADMISSION #17

Admit that you cannot provide documents proving [PLAINTIFF ANME HERE] owns this debt.

ADMISSION #18

Admit that your complaint is time barred in Georgia under Statute of Limitations. (See your states statute of limitations on credit card debts).

DOCUMENTS TO BE PRODUCED

STICK IT TO SUE HAPPY DEBT COLLECTORS

1. Provide the actual credit card contract upon which your Complaint is based on.

2. Provide a contract, agreement, assignment, or other means of demonstrating that the Plaintiff has the authority and was legally entitled to collect on the alleged debt.

3. Furnish reasonable proof, such as an original, or copies of the assignment agreement or assignment agreements, transferring the alleged contract and/or account in question from [ORIGINAL CREDITOR NAME HERE] over to [PLAINTIFF NAME HERE] to show an Assignment has been made and that [PLAINTIFF NAME HERE] are the real party in interest.

4. Provide a copy of the Assignment between [PLAINTIFF NAME HERE] and [ORIGINAL CREDITOR NAME HERE].

5. Provide evidence or proof of the Defendant's alleged debt to Plaintiff, including specifically the alleged contract, between the plaintiff and defendant or any other instrument constructed solely for the purpose of creating a loan agreement between the Plaintiff and Defendant bearing Defendants signature and/or Please Produce the contract that legally requires the Defendant to pay the amount entered into complaint.

DEBT BUYER (JUNK DEBT COLLECTORS) LAWSUITS

6. Provide the original or copy of the account agreement that states interest rate, grace period, finance charge, assignment, and specifically the State Laws that the agreement and account are governed plus other important facts.

7. Provide copies of the amount paid and/or the consideration due for the alleged contract/ account.

8. Provide an Itemized account of all transactions mentioned in Interrogatory Number Eighteen (18).

9. Provide the Record of Assignment that displays the information in Interrogatory No. 22.

10. Provide all copies of manuals, procedures, and protocols used by Plaintiff regarding communication with [ORIGINAL CREDITOR] regarding purchased debt.

11. Provide evidence of authorization of Plaintiff to do business, create loans, issue or extend credit, collect debts and/or operate in the State where the Plaintiff conducts their business.

12. Provide evidence of authorization of Plaintiff and Attorney to do business, create loans, issue or extend credit, collect debts

and/or operate as a financial business in the State of [YOUR STATE HERE].

13. Provide a document or documents(s) that proves you did send the defendant a notification of assignment of the account or assignment of rights.

14. Attach any and all notices sent to Defendant by Plaintiff in regards to this account demanding payment.

15. Attach copies of all statements generated while this alleged account was open with Plaintiff.

16. Attach a complete and accurate history of the interest charged on this alleged account with Plaintiff. Show the exact dates those interest rates changed and list the various rates that were charged during the this debt and the exact method of amortization.

17. Attach any and all notices sent to Defendant by Plaintiff announcing changes in interest, fees or penalties and/or the terms of this alleged debt.

18. Identify each Credit Reporting Agency (credit bureau) to which the Plaintiff reported defendant's debt and the dates of each such report.

19. Provide the original dunning letter that was sent to Defendant.

20. Attach any and all notices sent to Defendant by Plaintiff in regards to account announcing transfer and/or assignment of credit card account from plaintiff to any collection agency or collection attorney.

21. Attach a copy of the agreement with Plaintiff that grants [ATTORNEYS NAME HERE] Attorney(s) the authority to collect this alleged debt.

CERTIFICATE OF SERVICE

I hereby certify that a copy of the foregoing Requests for Discovery was mailed on the [DATE: Day, Month, YEAR to [ATTORNEY NAME AND ADDRESS].

_____
Defendant Pro Se

[YOUR ADDRESS, CITY, STATE, ZIP]
[YOUR PHONE NUMBER]

[NOTARY PUBLIC]

Definition of Subpoena Duces Tectum

Subpoena duces tecum (from Discovery Instructions); Latin for: Bring with thee. A writ commonly called a Subpoena Duces Tecum, commanding the person to whom it is directed to bring with him some writings, papers, or other things therein specified and described, to a deposition, to counsel for litigants in an action, or before the court. ~ LectLaw.com

DEBT BUYER (JUNK DEBT COLLECTORS) LAWSUITS

In general, all relevant papers in the possession of the witness must be produced, but to this general rule there are exceptions. E.g., attorneys and solicitors who hold the papers of their clients cannot be compelled to produce them, unless the client could have been so compelled; neither can documents that are covered by the 5th Amendment's protection against self-incrimination.

RESPONSES TO PLAINTIFFS DISCOVERY

When you file your discovery requests you can bet that the opposing attorney will file discovery for you to answer, admit and produce. Be extremely careful how you answer the interrogatories, admissions and production of documents. Never state: "lack of information", it will leave you open to filing a motion with the court to deem your admission admitted. Don't worry I will show you how to avoid that trap

See Responses to Discovery in Chapter Three. It covers information that I use in both original creditor and junk debt buyer Discovery responses (Interrogatories, Admissions, and Requests for Documents). This is the same whether it is an original creditor or junk debt buyer lawsuit.

5

DEALING WITH DEBT COLLECTORS BEFORE THEY SUE YOU

Let's face, it the Federal Trade Commission is useless on an individual level, and by the time action is brought by the FTC against a debt collector many consumers have already been hurt. However, with that being said we can use the Fair Debt Collection Practices Act (FDCPA – U.S.C Title 15) and sue bad debt collectors.

If you, or someone you know, are having problems with creditors or collection agencies, this is the chapter that ALL debt collectors hope you never read.

Severe economic times, including lay-offs, slowdowns, or losing a job, medical problems, and divorce can put you in financial

DEALING WITH DEBT COLLECTORS BEFORE THEY SUE YOU

peril. After getting behind a couple of months, the collectors will inevitably start calling and harassing you.

If debt collectors are harassing you, I feel your pain, and I have walked in the same shoes. I'm not afraid to admit I've had financial problems, and I want to help others that have to endure the same issues and abuse that I have. Just remember, it's not the end of the world and there are certain things you can do to reduce or stop the harassment.

I've had my share of struggling with debt and dealing with creditors and debt collectors. In the past, I would get depressed over it. Of course, the idiots calling from collection agencies just don't seem to understand that no matter what they say or threaten, they aren't going to get paid until I am able. I've seen and heard it all. I've been threatened with "criminal lawsuits" which, is of course illegal. They have attempted to shame me and/or intimidate me. Believe it or not, they've even threatened to call neighbors and worse, actually do it, which of course is illegal.

STICK IT TO SUE HAPPY DEBT COLLECTORS

So far, all but two collection agencies that have come after me have used illegal, unethical and underhanded tricks in their attempt to collect. So what can you do about such shameless behavior?

First calm down, there is hope, and being behind on your debts is only temporary if you work on getting out of debt.

The second thing you should remember above all else, is to pay your necessities first (house, food, utilities, vehicle, insurance, clothing, etc). These should always come before you consider paying debts you have fallen behind on. Many debt collectors will try to get you to make a payment, even when you only have enough to cover your basic needs. Don't listen to them, pay your necessities first.

If you have anything left over after paying your basic needs then divide what's left up between the companies and people you owe. See further down this post for an illustration of how to divide money between creditors based on what you owe.

If the debt collectors are ringing your phone off the hook, there are several things you can do to lessen and even stop it. I am not sure why debt collectors think that by being abusive it is going

DEALING WITH DEBT COLLECTORS BEFORE THEY SUE YOU

to help matters. I've heard that they try to make you upset and angry because you are more than likely going to pay them something just to shut them up. Don't fall for it, their only purpose is to extract money from you, and they will trick, lie, embarrass, and harass you to get what they want. They are not your friends, don't listen to them.

If at all possible, record all debt collection phone calls. Many answering machines have a record function, use it whenever possible.

Secondly, if a collector gets abusive or starts yelling, tell them that if they continue with that behavior you will hang up, and if they continue then hang up. They will probably call back, if they do remain calm and answer the phone (or let it go to the answering machine), if you choose to answer the phone and they again become abusive or start yelling, calmly tell them that until they calm down and stop misbehaving, you are not going to talk to them and hang up. You take their "power" away from them when you remain calm and tell them you aren't going to discuss anything until they calm down.

STICK IT TO SUE HAPPY DEBT COLLECTORS

If they are calling your place of employment you can write them a "Cease and Desist" telephone communication letter, be sure to send it certified mail with return receipt so you know they received it (this may come in handy if they violate the Cease and Desist letter). As soon as the first call hits where I work, I write a simple Cease and Desist letter (see example below) and send it certified mail. More than 90% of the collectors will stop calling after receiving such a letter. A collector can call once after receiving such a letter but that's it, if they call more than that they are in violation of the Fair Debt Collections Practices Act (FDCPA) and you can report them to the Federal Trade Commission (www.fTC.gov) and file suit against them. I let them violate the do not call a couple of times and then file a FDCPA lawsuit against them. I'll show you the basics of how to file FDCPA violation lawsuits in this chapter.

I've had several collectors violate the FDCPA by calling repeatedly after receiving my Cease and Desist letter. Currently one is trying to settle with me out of court for violating the FDCPA and the other two I have filed lawsuits against them for their illegal behavior. I have all of the recorded phone conversations, photos of the caller ID and the return receipt card they signed when they

DEALING WITH DEBT COLLECTORS BEFORE THEY SUE YOU

received my certified Cease and Desist calling letter. There are 37 states that allow one party (one person) consent to record a telephone call (see link at end of this article). Additionally, if they are calling your employer and you record it you may be okay as it is at your place of employment you have no reasonable expectancy of privacy, so it would hold up in court even if the person calling you is in a two party consent state."

I've also had success in filing complaints with the Federal Trade Commission (www.ftc.gov) and the Better Business Bureau (www.bbb.org). It seems that even the most unscrupulous debt collectors will back off once they know you will complain about their unethical practices. The FTC takes abusive collections practices seriously, so be sure to report all violations to them (www.ftc.gov).

Write down each time a collector calls and keep track of this, keep copies of all your certified letters and return receipts from your Cease and Desist letters, save those phone recordings, you never know when you will need them.

STICK IT TO SUE HAPPY DEBT COLLECTORS

Only agree to talk to a debt collection company or creditor once every two weeks, if they call more than that, tell them that they have already called in the last two weeks and you will not speak with them again until the next two week period, then politely tell them you are ending the call.

You can send a letter to Cease and Desist for ALL telephone communications. However, this could trigger them filing a lawsuit (Though not likely on debts under $2,000.00). This is a judgment call on your part. If the collector is very abusive then this may be an avenue you want to take.

---- **SAMPLE CEASE CALLING LETTER** ---

[DATE]

[YOUR NAME AND ADDRESS]

[DEBT COLLECTORS NAME AND ADDRESS]

RE: Regarding calls to employer [ADD ANY REFERENCE NUMBERS FROM DEBT COLLECTOR HERE]

Dear [INSERT DEBT COLLECTION COMPANY NAME HERE],

DEALING WITH DEBT COLLECTORS BEFORE THEY SUE YOU

I am writing to formally request that your firm (or any agency hired by your firm) no longer contact me at my place of employment, [INSERT YOUR EMPLOYER HERE AND PHONE NUMBER(S)].

My employer requests that calls such as yours must cease, under the terms of the 1977 Federal Fair Debt Collection Practices Act, I formally demand all such calls to my place of employment cease. You will take note that this letter was mailed certified mail, so I have proof that you are in receipt of this letter should legal action against you become necessary on this matter.

Please give this matter the attention that it deserves.

Sincerely,

[SIGN HERE]

--- END OF SAMPLE CEASE CALLING LETTER ---

The NeverS and Always Tips for Dealing with Debt Collectors

These "Never" and "Always" tips are primarily aimed at consumers that are having financial difficulties and cannot pay their debts as agreed with their creditors.

The "Nevers"

NEVER get emotional when talking to a debt collector on the phone.

Debt collectors will attempt to evoke strong emotion from you (anger, outrage, frustration, guilt, fear etc.). Many collectors use this method in an attempt to cause you to think irrationally. Their hope is to make you become very emotional, it is then that they can most often get you to agree to something you most likely would never have agreed to had you not been in a state of mental distress. Don't trust them, they will do anything (lie, slander, threaten legal action, etc.) to get paid.

This trick works well and they WILL try to use it, so don't fall for it. Always remain calm when dealing with a collector on the phone.

DEALING WITH DEBT COLLECTORS BEFORE THEY SUE YOU

If they become abusive, calmly state that you are not going to discuss the matter further until they calm down, tell them if they continue then you will hang up. Chances are they will yell and scream some more. When they do start yelling or abuse you, simply hang up. They will undoubtedly call you back. If they again become abusive or start yelling, remain calm and repeat that you will not discuss the matter until they calm down, if they don't calm down then hang up again. Repeat this as often as necessary.

NEVER under any circumstance give a debt collector or collection agency your bank account information, checking account number, or debit card number to draft your account. Always pay by money order or cashier's check.

Many times the collection agency will draft your account for more than the agreed upon amount, thus over drafting your account. They may also draft your account multiple times. You would not give a total stranger walking down the street your bank account information, so don't give a debt collector your banking information. Often the collector will say they must have your payment by the end of the day and moan and groan.

STICK IT TO SUE HAPPY DEBT COLLECTORS

Tell them you will send them a cashier's check or money order. They will try and object, tell them if they want to be paid they will accept a check or money order. If you remain firm, they will accept this.

You are already in debt, so what if the collector doesn't get his money immediately, they can get their money in a few days. Be sure to get the check or money order in the mail as soon as possible.

DO NOT BUDGE ON THIS. I have read literally hundreds stories of people that have had their bank accounts raped by unscrupulous debt collection agencies.

NEVER let a debt collector set the terms of a repayment agreement.

You know what you can afford to pay, the debt collector doesn't. They will try their best to get the most money possible from you. You decide what you can afford to pay. Most debt collectors are compensated based on their performance, so naturally they will try to take as much as they can. Make sure you can cover your basic living necessities then arrange payments with what you have left.

DEALING WITH DEBT COLLECTORS BEFORE THEY SUE YOU

NEVER take any form of verbal or emotional abuse from a debt collector.

You are a human being and no person has the right to strip you of your dignity. If they abuse you verbally, remain calm and tell them that until they change their attitude you will not discuss the matter with them, and threaten to hang up the phone. If they continue their abuse, exercise your right to hang up. There are no laws on the books that require you to talk to a debt collector on the phone. They may try to tell you otherwise, but don't believe them.

The Always

ALWAYS have the debt collector put the payment arrangements in writing.

Don't pay a single cent until you get the agreed upon arrangement in writing. The collector may moan and groan about it. Tell them if they want to be paid you MUST have the arrangements in writing. This is to protect you in case the collection agency tries to change the terms of the agreement or tries anything underhanded. When you receive the agreement, be sure to read over it thoroughly to make sure they haven't slipped anything into the agreement that wasn't agreed to by you. If they have added terms to the agreement call them and tell them what you received is not what you discussed or agreed to. Tell them to send it back corrected. DO NOT BUDGE ON THIS.

ALWAYS record the telephone conversation; even they are calling from a two party consent state, record the conversation. If they are calling from a one party state, you DO NOT have to tell them you are recording the conversation. If they are being abusive, tell them you are recording the conversation. They will either change their tone or hang up on you.

BE SNEAKY, use their own methods against them, especially if the debt collector is calling from a two party consent* state. When they read off their script, "this call may be recorded for", say (in a humorous and joking way) "I am recording this call for customer service reasons", they won't think about it and probably think you are joking, however by them not saying "NO" they are giving consent for you to record the conversation.

*Several states require the consent of both parties of a telephone conversion in order to allow the call to be recorded. 37 states

DEALING WITH DEBT COLLECTORS BEFORE THEY SUE YOU

allow the consent of just ONE party (i.e. you don't have to disclose that you are recording the conversation). If you are at work, neither you nor they have any reasonable expectancy of privacy, so if a collector calls you at work you still may be able to record the conversation without violating any state or federal law.

NOTE: If the debt collectors phone number doesn't show up on the caller ID or displays "unknown", you should then you have every right to assume that they are calling from a one party state, because they are attempting to hide their location. A Federal Trade Commission staff attorney disclosed this to me.

REMEMBER

ALWAYS keep a record of every phone call and postal mail contact from all collection agencies.

Be sure to write down the time, date, the name of person that contacted you, the company and any phone numbers.

ALWAYS pay exactly what you agreed to pay, when you agreed to pay it. Fair is fair, you owe the money and for some reason got behind on paying the creditor.

ALWAYS remain calm when talking with a debt collector on the phone.

ALWAYS attempt to negotiate the amount unless you are financially able to pay back the debt fully.

More often than not, the collection agency bought your debt from your creditor. They buy the debt at a discount (so many cents per dollar owed). Which means many times the collector will take less than face value on the debt. The collector will of course try to get as much as they can, if they see you won't budge they will often drop the amount you must pay back. If you are financially able to pay the debt, and then pay it, after all you owe the debt. If you aren't in a good financial situation try negotiating.

Always get any negotiated amount in writing from the collection agency, do not pay a single dime until you receive it, and read it over thoroughly before making any payments.

ALWAYS pay what you agreed to pay.

You owe the money, you gave your word, so pay it per the agreed upon terms. Pay the debt as agreed and in a timely man-

DEALING WITH DEBT COLLECTORS BEFORE THEY SUE YOU

ner. You never know when you might have more financial problems and need to discuss different payment arrangements with the collector.

How to Pay Collection Agencies or Creditors

How to pay collection agencies or creditors with money left over after you pay your necessities.

Let's say you have outstanding debt that equals $2,000.00 and you have $100.00 left over after you paid for your families basic necessities.

Major Credit Card	$1500.00
Retail Store Credit Card	$ 250.00
Retail Store Credit Card	$ 250.00
Total	**$2,000.00**

What you want to do is divide the $100.00 you have to pay debt with based on the percentage you owe each creditor.

Since 75% of your debt is owed to the Major Credit Card, you would pay them $75.00 of the $100.00 and $12.50 to each of the other two (as they are 12.5 % of the debt, so they get to split the other $25.00 of your extra money).

Call each creditor or collection agency and tell them what you are paying and why you are paying it the way you are (the percentage pay off as outlined above). You'll find that if you call them each time you make a payment, they will call you less. This puts the "power" back on your side. Freak them out by calling them.

If you don't have much left after paying your necessities, pay what you can on the biggest debts and the others can wait until the next time you have extra money to pay down the debts. If a creditor or collection company calls because you didn't make a payment, tell them that you only had so much money to pay debts with and that they fell below the line this month, and that you will do your best to make a payment next month, if there is any money to do so. Take the initiative, call the creditors that you won't be paying this month, and tell them that unfortunately there is not money to pay them this month, perhaps next month. Debt collectors just don't know what to do in cases such as this. Mess with their heads!

DEALING WITH DEBT COLLECTORS BEFORE THEY SUE YOU

Always be polite and do not take any form of abuse form them, again, if they become abusive tell them that you aren't going to talk to them until they calm down and tell them that you are now hanging up. No one deserves to be abused, threatened or intimidated by anyone else. Don't accept it.

Do what you have to do to make extra money to pay your debts. Get an extra job, sell stuff (after all it is only stuff, you can buy it again when you are out of debt), have a yard sale, anything to make money to pay off those debts. If you work hard, then the situation is only temporary. The faster you work to get the debts paid off the faster it all goes away.

How to Sue Debt Collectors for violations of the FDCPA or FCRA

You don't need an attorney to start a FDCPA lawsuit. You can always get one involved once it gets on the court docket.

Backgrounder

#1 - Log everything like debt collector calls, demand letters, etc. Date/time and who it is. Be vigilant.

#2 - Take pictures of the CallerID (if you don't have it get it), save and print these out and put them in a file. I keep one on each debt collector that has or is contacting me so I can keep it organized.

#3 - Record all telephone conversations. If you live in a one-party state (such as Georgia) and the debt collector is calling from a one-party consent state you don't have to advise them that you are recording the call. An easy way to get around two-party consent state calls is once the debt collector tells you that they call is being recording, jokingly say yes I am too (do it in a humorous or off-hand way), if they don't object you are good to go.

Save the phone calls and burn them to a disc or discs, I save them until I file suit.

#4 - When you get the initial written communication from the debt collector, send them a certified letter disputing the debt and request validation of the debt (this is the point most often where the debt collector will screw up, especially those that bought the debt from the original creditor or from another debt buyer that sold the account to them). They cannot continue to collect until they satisfy your request for validation. If they do then you have at least one FDCPA violation and could ultimately get a case thrown out if they choose to sue you.

#5 - Publicize the debt collectors bad behavior. Let other consumers in on information and more importantly, let the debt collection company know that you don't have a problem telling the world what they are doing. Blog about it, post on consumer complaint forums, contact sites such as Consumerist.com, call your local newspaper or other large newspaper and TV news in your area or state. Let them feel some of the same "heat" they are putting on you.

#6 - If the debt collector is calling your cell phone and you answer and you hear a moment of dead silence then they are using an automated dialer and that is a violation of the TCPA (Telephone Consumer Protection Act) in addition to the possibility of them violating the FDCPA.

When I send a dispute/validation request I also demand they Cease and Desist all telephone communications. 99.9% of the time they will violate it and you have a FDCPA violation to sue them for. Send your dispute, validation, cease telephone communications letter via certified mail so you have a record that they received it.

#7 - Always file a FDCPA violation complaint against the Debt Collector for each violation with the Federal Trade Commission (www.ftc.gov).

What Debt Collectors CANNOT do (Federal Title 15 U.S.C. 1692 FDCPA violations) ~ *About.com*

Ask you to pay more than you owe, the collector cannot misrepresent the amount you owe. [15 USC 1692e] § 807(2)(a)

Ask you to pay interest, fees, or expenses that are not allowed by law

The collector can't add on any extra fees that your original credit or loan agreement doesn't allow. [15 USC 1692f] § 808(1).

Call repeatedly or continuously - The FDCPA considers repeat calls as harassment. [15 USC 1692d] § 806(5).

Use obscene, profane, or abusive language - Using this kind of language is considered harassment. [15 USC 1692d] § 806(2).

DEALING WITH DEBT COLLECTORS BEFORE THEY SUE YOU

Call before 8:00 am or after 9:00 pm - Calls during these times are considered harassment. [15 USC 1692c] § 805(a)(1).

Calls at times the collector knew or should know are inconvenient - Calls at these times are considered harassment. [15 USC 1692c] § 805(a)(1).

Use or threaten to use violence if you don't pay the debt - Collectors can't threaten violence against you. [15 USC 1692d] § 806(1).

Threaten action they cannot or will not take. Collectors can't threaten to sue or file charges against you, garnish wages, take property, cause job loss, or ruin your credit when the collector cannot or does not intend to take the action. [15 USC 1692e] § 807(5).

Illegally inform a third party about your alleged debt. Unless you have expressly given permission, collectors are not allowed to inform anyone about your debt except:

- Your attorney
- The creditor
- The creditor's attorney

- A credit reporting agency
- Your spouse
- Your parent (if you are a minor)

[15 USC 1692c] § 805(b).

Repeatedly call a third party to get your location information. A collector can only contact a third party once unless it has reason to believe the information previously provided is false. [15 USC 1692b] § 804(1)

Unless the debt collector has your permission they cannot contact you at your place of employment.

Initial Steps in filing FDCPA lawsuits

#1 - Read the Fair Debt Collections Practices Act and familiarize yourself with the sections and chapters that cover debt collector violations (1692a-k). While you are working on this I suggest you locate and employ a consumer protection or consumer law attorney, you can find one in your state at www.naca.net and www.martindale.com. Consumer protection attorney's generally don't charge any upfront fees and only get paid when you win your case against the debt collector.

DEALING WITH DEBT COLLECTORS BEFORE THEY SUE YOU

#2 - The Fair Debt Collection Practices Act allows you to file suit in just about any court in the US, such as small claims court, state court and of course federal court. I generally start at the state court level and let the debt collecting defendant remove it to federal court if they want. More than likely they will so they can invoke an Offer of compromise. Good for them, when they move it to federal court you can bet the Federal Trade Commission can gain access to more evidence of their bad behavior if and when they decide to investigate the debt collector. Of course the Federal Trade Commission seems to move at glacier speed when spanking bad debt collectors (maybe this will change one day). You can file a FDCPA suit in the county you live in, even though the defendant is not located in your county or state.

#3 - Check your states procedures on serving a company, most state's laws (code) are online and will give you the information on how to properly serve.

For instance in the State of Georgia proper service of a foreign corporation is as follows:

STICK IT TO SUE HAPPY DEBT COLLECTORS

O.C.G.A. § 14-2-1510 Foreign Corporations - service.

(a) The registered agent of a foreign corporation authorized to transact business in this state is the corporation's agent for service of process, notice, or demand required or permitted by law to be served on the foreign corporation.

(b) If a foreign corporation has no registered agent or its registered agent cannot with reasonable diligence be served, the corporation may be served by registered or certified mail or statutory overnight delivery, return receipt requested, addressed to the chief executive officer, chief financial officer, or secretary of the foreign corporation, or a person holding a position comparable to any of the foregoing, at its principal office shown in the later of its application for a certificate of authority or its most recent annual registration. Any party that serves a foreign corporation in accordance with this subsection shall also serve a copy of the process upon the Secretary of State and shall pay a $10.00 filing fee.

(c) Service is perfected under subsection (b) of this Code section at the earliest of:

(1) The date the foreign corporation receives the mail;

DEALING WITH DEBT COLLECTORS BEFORE THEY SUE YOU

(2) The date shown on the return receipt, if signed on behalf of the foreign corporation; or

(3) Five days after its deposit in the United States mail, as evidenced by the postmark, if mailed postpaid and correctly addressed.

(d) This Code section does not prescribe the only means, or necessarily the required means, of serving a foreign corporation.

Also see O.C.G.A. § 14-9-902.1

You can search your states Secretary of State's website, or contact them to find the registered agent. Of course this is mainly for out of state defendants, however if you are filing against a debt collector in your state you will still need to serve the corporations registered agent.

Each state has different rules and regulations on proper service so be sure to check with your state laws to ensure you don't serve it incorrectly.

In State Lawsuits

Once you know who the registered agent is, it will display the county in which they are located. Make a note of it, as you will need this when filing/serving.

Search the Sheriff's office website (for the county the registered agents is located in) and find the civil service section (or call them if they don't have one). Find out what you need to send to them for serving the registered agent. Usually it is a copy of the suit (sometimes they require two original copies) (aka process to serve), a check made out to them for the service fee (money orders are generally acceptable), a Sheriff's Entry of Service (get it from your court clerk's office when filing) and a self addressed self stamped envelope (SASE) so you can get your copies back). Remember once you get your copies back you'll need to file one with your court clerk's office and then the 30 day clock starts ticking for the defendant to reply with an answer to you suit.

Draft your FDCPA violations civil complaint (I will post references and samples very soon, so check back here often) and my advice is to make 6 original copies and get them all notarized as required by law. Take them to the court clerk's office along with the filing fee. Once it is filed, ask the court clerk for a

DEALING WITH DEBT COLLECTORS BEFORE THEY SUE YOU

couple of "Sheriff's Entry of Service" forms (one for each defendant and extras in case you make a typo). I recommend when filing the complaint to demand a jury trial, juries *LOVE* awarding big damages in FDCPA lawsuits.

Then follow the directions for serving the registered agent in the county they reside in.

YOU JUST SUED A DEBT COLLECTOR!

If you start stressing or feel like you are over your head when things start heating up in court, get a consumer protection advocate (generally free) or a consumer law attorney involved. You can do this at *any* time during the suing process.

About 95% of the time the debt collector will attempt to settle with you before the case goes to trial. Demand everything they wish to settle in writing, if they won't give it you in writing, politely tell them "we will just have to see each other in court".

NOTE #1

After they answer (if they do) you may receive a "notice of removal" this just means they are moving the case to a higher court, most likely U.S. Federal District Court. I like federal court better than state court, the rule of procedure are clearer and easier for "no lawyer types" like me to understand.

Just remember you have rights as a consumer and as a human being, don't let *anyone* abuse those rights. Put those corrupt debt collectors where they belong, behind the defendants table in court. It's time to fight back against abusive and illegal debt collection tactics. The more consumers who do this, the less likely these companies will continue their abusive behavior.

NOTE #2

If you are dealing with a 3rd party debt collector or debt buyer, just remember all evidence they provide or testimony they make is 100% hearsay.

Fair Credit Reporting Act (FCRA) Violations

If you are having financial difficulties I would suggest that you freeze your credit with each of the three credit reporting companies. The reason is that many times a debt collection law firm will pull your credit reports and then file a lawsuit against you. This is illegal as litigation is not permissible use to access a consumer's credit because it does not involve a business to consumer transaction (such as applying for credit). You can sue

DEALING WITH DEBT COLLECTORS BEFORE THEY SUE YOU

a law firm or debt collector that pulls your credit report and then subsequently files suit against you.

> In the 1990 Commentary on the FCRA, the Federal Trade Commission ("Commission") stated that "[t]he possibility that a party may be involved in litigation involving a consumer does not provide a permissible purpose for that party to receive a consumer report on such consumer . . . because litigation is not a 'business transaction' involving the consumer." 16 C.F.R. § 600 App., 55 Fed. Reg. 18804, 18816 (May 4, 1990). This statement extends to all aspects of litigation, including the pre-litigation discussions and settlement preparations that you describe, and was not altered by the recent amendments to the statute. – *Federal Trade Commission FCRA Staff Opinion: Cosgrove-Greenblatt*

Before I wised up I found law firm inquires on my credit report right just before they filed suit. I filed suit against them for violating the FCRA (and for FDCPA violations). They subsequently dropped their lawsuit and at the time of this writing my suit is still pending.

STICK IT TO SUE HAPPY DEBT COLLECTORS

For most consumers it only costs about ten dollars ($10.00) per reporting agency to freeze your credit. You can often freeze your credit using an online form. One agency does require you to send them postal mail along with a check or credit card/debit card number.

The three credit reporting agencies are: Experian, Equifax and TransUnion. You can find the proper procedure for freezing your credit on their websites.

Experian - www.experian.com

Equifax - www.equifax.com

TransUnion - www.transunion.com

The example on the following page can be used in Federal District Court and in most state courts.

DEALING WITH DEBT COLLECTORS BEFORE THEY SUE YOU

IN THE STATE COURT OF [YOUR COUNTY] COUNTY
STATE OF [YOUR STATE]

[YOUR NAME],	)	
	)	
	)	Case No.:
	)	
Plaintiff,	)	
	)	
	)	
vs.	)	
	)	
	)	
[PLAINTIFFS NAME HERE]	)	

Defendant

COMPLAINT AND DEMAND FOR JURY TRIAL

I. INTRODUCTION

This is an action for damages brought by an individual consumer for Defendant's violations of the Fair Debt Collection Practices Act, 15 U.S.C. § 1692, et seq. (hereinafter "FDCPA"), which prohibit debt collectors from engaging in abusive, deceptive, and unfair practices.

STICK IT TO SUE HAPPY DEBT COLLECTORS

II. JURISDICTION AND VENUE

Jurisdiction of this Court arises under 15 U.S.C. § 1692k(d) and 28 U.S.C. § 1337. Declaratory relief is available pursuant to 28 U.S.C. §§ 2201 and 2202 Venue in this District is proper in that the defendants transact business here and the conduct complained of occurred here.

III. PARTIES

Plaintiff, [YOUR NAME], is a natural person residing in the state of [YOUR STATE]. Defendant, [PLAINTIFF NAME], is a corporation engaged in the business of collecting debts in this state with its principal place of business located at [PLAINTIFF FULL MAILING ADDRESS]. The principal purpose of Defendant is the collection of debts using the mails and telephone, and Defendant regularly attempts to collect debts alleged to be due another.

Defendant, John Doe, is a natural person employed by Defendant as a collector at all times relevant to this complaint.

DEALING WITH DEBT COLLECTORS BEFORE THEY SUE YOU

Defendants are "debt collectors" as defined by the FDCPA, 15 U.S.C. § 1692a(6).

IV. FACTUAL ALLEGATIONS

[This paragraph below is for illustration only to give you an idea how to word the complaint, replace the information to suit your own needs]

On or about November 4, 2008, Defendant, while employed as a collector by Defendant, contacted Plaintiff's employer, and requested Plaintiff's employer to speak to Plaintiff regarding the importance of paying alleged debts. Plaintiff's employer informed Plaintiff of this contact. On or about July 29, 2008 Plaintiff wrote requesting Defendants not to contact Plaintiff's employer or otherwise contact Plaintiff via telephone communications. On or about November 19, 2008 Plaintiff filed a complaint with the Better Business Bureau requesting Defendants not to contact Plaintiff's employer. As a result of the acts alleged above, Plaintiff suffered headaches, nausea, embarrassment, mental depression and emotional distress, lost weight, interruption of work, lost time, and expenses.

V. CLAIM FOR RELIEF

Plaintiff repeats and realleges and incorporates by reference paragraphs one through four above. Defendants violated the FDCPA. Defendants' violations include, but are not limited to, the following: (a) The Defendants violated 15 U.S.C. § 1692c(b) by contacting a third party, the Plaintiff's employer, without the Plaintiff's prior consent. (b) The Defendants violated 15 U.S.C. § 1692c(c) by contacting the Plaintiff after the Plaintiff had requested the Defendants cease communication with the Plaintiff. (c) The Defendants violated 15 U.S.C. § 1692g(b) by failing to provide verification of the debt and continuing its debt collection efforts after the plaintiff had disputed the debt in writing within thirty days of receiving notice of the 15 U.S.C. § 1692g debt validation rights. As a result of the above violations of the FDCPA, the Defendants are liable to the Plaintiff for declaratory judgment that defendants' conduct violated the FDCPA, injunc-

DEALING WITH DEBT COLLECTORS BEFORE THEY SUE YOU

tive relief, and Plaintiff's actual damages, statutory damages, and costs and attorney's fees.

WHEREFORE, Plaintiff respectfully prays that judgment be entered against the Defendant for the following:

A. Declaratory judgment that defendants' conduct violated the FDCPA and injunctive relief for the defendants' violations;

B. Actual damages;

C. Statutory damages pursuant to 15 U.S.C. § 1692k.;

D. Costs and reasonable attorney's fees pursuant to 15 U.S.C. § 1692k.;

E. For such other and further relief as may be just and proper.

DEMAND FOR JURY TRIAL

Please take notice that Plaintiff demands trial by jury in this action.

STICK IT TO SUE HAPPY DEBT COLLECTORS

_____

Plaintiff

Dated this April 1, 2009

VERIFICATION

I [YOUR NAME] hereby certify that the facts contained in the foregoing Complaint are true and correct to the best of my knowledge, information and belief.

_____

[YOURNAME] – *pro se*

[NOTARY PUBLIC]

REMEMBER: In most states you will need to obtain and order of entry and a summons from the court clerk that must be served upon the defendant along with the complaint. If the defendant is a corporation (i.e a law firm) you will need to check with your secretary of state's office to find out who their registered agent

DEALING WITH DEBT COLLECTORS BEFORE THEY SUE YOU

is. You must serve the registered agent of the law firm/company.

DISCLAIMER

This book is offered to the User conditionally on acceptance by the User without modification of the terms, conditions, and notices contained herein. Use of the content presented in book constitutes the User's agreement to abide by the following terms and conditions. This book is for informational purposes only and may not in any way, shape, or form be construed as legal advice.

Copyright Notices

All contents of this book are Copyright © 2009, Allen Harkleroad, All rights reserved. Reproduction in whole or in part without permission is prohibited.

Disclaimer

ALL MATERIALS INCLUDED IN THIS BOOK ARE PROVIDED "AS IS" WITHOUT WARRANTY OF ANY KIND. THE CONTENT PUBLISHED MAY INCLUDE INACCURACIES OR TYPOGRAPHICAL ERRORS. CHANGES ARE PERIODICALLY MADE TO THE INFORMATION HEREIN. ALLEN HARKLEROAD MAY MAKE IMPROVEMENTS AND/OR CHANGES TO THE BOOK AT ANY TIME. ALLEN HARKLEROAD MAKE NO REPRESENTATIONS AND, TO THE FULLEST EXTENT ALLOWED BY LAW DISCLAIM ALL WARRANTIES,

EXPRESS OR IMPLIED, INCLUDING, BUT NOT LIMITED TO WARRANTIES OF MERCHANTABILITY AND FITNESS FOR A PARTICULAR PURPOSE REGARDING THE SUITABILITY OF THE INFORMATION; THE ACCURACY, RELIABILITY, COMPLETENESS OR TIMELINESS OF THE CONTENT, SERVICES, PRODUCTS, TEXT, GRAPHICS, LINKS, OR OTHER ITEMS CONTAINED WITHIN THE BOOK, OR THE RESULTS OBTAINED FROM ACCESSING AND USING THIS BOOK AND/OR THE CONTENT CONTAINED HEREIN. ALLEN HARKLEROAD DOES NOT WARRANT THAT THE FUNCTIONS CONTAINED IN THE MATERIALS WILL BE UNINTERRUPTED OR ERROR-FREE, THAT DEFECTS WILL BE CORRECTED. Use of this book is at your own risk.

This book may contain advice, opinions, and statements of various information providers and content providers. Allen Harkleroad does not represent or endorse the accuracy or reliability of any advice, opinion, statement or other information provided by any information provider or content provider, or any user of this site or other person or entity. Reliance upon any such opinion, advice, statement, or other information shall also be at your own risk. Neither Allen Harkleroad or his affiliates, nor any of their respective agents, employees, information providers or content providers shall be liable to any User or anyone else for any inaccuracy, error, omission, interruption, timeliness, completeness, deletion, defect, failure of performance, alteration of, or use of any content herein, regardless of cause, for any damages resulting therefrom. Allen Harkleroad, his affiliates, information providers and his content providers shall not have any liability for investment or legal decisions based upon, or the results obtained from, the information provided. Allen Harkleroad, his affiliates, information providers and content providers do not guarantee or warrant the timeliness, sequence, accuracy, or completeness of any such information. Nothing contained in this book is intended to be, nor shall it be construed as investment or legal advice.

User agrees to indemnify and hold harmless Allen Harkleroad and all officers, directors, shareholders, employees, authorized representatives and agents form and against all claims and expenses, including attorneys' fees, arising out of any use or misuse of information contained in this book .

Modification

Allen Harkleroad shall have the right, at its discretion, to change, modify, add, or remove terms of this agreement at any time. Notification of any such changes shall be made herein. Changes shall be effective immediately, and subsequent use by you of this site shall constitute your acceptance of them.

Termination

This agreement is effective until terminated by Allen Harkleroad, at any time without notice.

Indemnity/Limitation of Liability

Under no circumstances, including, but not limited to, negligence, shall Allen Harkleroad, or his affiliates be liable for any direct, indirect, incidental, special or consequential damages that result from the use of, or the inability to use the information contained in this book. As a condition of use of this book, the User agrees to indemnify Allen Harkleroad and his suppliers from and against any and all liabilities, expenses and damages arising out of claims resulting from User's use of this book, including without limitation any claims alleging facts that if true would constitute a breach by User of these terms and conditions. If you are dissatisfied with any the books material, or with any of books terms and conditions, your sole and exclusive remedy is to discontinue using the book.

General

Allen Harkleroad reserves the right to make any and all changes to this book at his sole discretion without notice to the User. This Agreement shall be deemed to include all other notices, policies, disclaimers, and other terms contained in this book; provided, however, that in the event of a conflict between such other terms and the terms of this Agreement, the terms of this Agreement shall control. This Agreement has been made in and shall be construed and enforced in accordance with Georgia law. Any action to enforce this agreement shall be brought in the federal or state courts located in Georgia. If any provision is deemed to be unlawful or unenforceable, that shall not affect the validity and enforceability of the remaining provisions.

Any rights not expressly granted herein are reserved

Made in the USA
Middletown, DE
23 February 2015